SPARKY!

Sparky Anderson
with
Dan Ewald

PRENTICE
HALL
PRESS

NEW YORK   LONDON   TORONTO   SYDNEY   TOKYO   SINGAPORE

PRENTICE HALL PRESS
15 Columbus Circle
New York, NY 10023

Library of Congress Cataloging-in-Publication Data

Anderson, Sparky, 1934–
Sparky! / Sparky Anderson, with Dan Ewald. — 1st Prentice Hall Press ed.
p.   cm.
ISBN 0-13-109463-7
1. Anderson, Sparky, 1934– . 2. Baseball—United States—
Managers—Biography. I. Ewald, Dan. II. Title.
GV865.A48A3   1990
796.357′092—dc20
[B]   89–48150
CIP

Designed by Irving Perkins Associates

Manufactured in the United States of America

10 9 8 7 6 5 4 3 2 1

First Edition

Contents

Winning 1

Going Home 13

Coming Back 27

Sparky 39

Growing Up 53

Managing 65

Managers 87

Casey 101

The World Series 111

Fired! 127

Success 143

Players, Past and Present 153

Impact Players and Clutch Players 165

Peter Edward Rose 179

All-Timers 191

Giants 207

Parks 219

Thank You 239

The Record 247

A Tribute, by Dan Ewald 251

Index 257

SPARKY!

Winning

My name is Sparky Anderson. And I'm a winaholic.

I'm not proud to have to admit it. It took twenty years in the big leagues and a nosedive crash into reality to finally figure it out.

But I am proud I am finally able to admit it. I'm even prouder to be taking steps to deal with a problem I've had all my life.

There's nothing wrong with wanting to win. There's nothing wrong with grinding your guts to do everything you can to make it happen.

There's something definitely wrong, though, when you take it to the point where winning becomes an obsession and hazardous to your health or the well-being of your family. That's when the urgency to win crosses over the line of sanity. That's when winning actually becomes a disease.

I've had to face that disease. The showdown came on May 19, 1989. That's the day I left the Tigers. I went home to Thousand Oaks, California, for seventeen days to recuperate from what was termed "exhaustion."

I was exhausted all right. Physically I could not have made it through another day. There was more, though. I also was mentally drained. My nerves were shot. I could not function.

There were all kinds of reasons for the condition I was in. With the demands of managing and commitments to charities, the media and a variety of other obligations, I was trying to cram forty-eight hours into a twenty-four-hour day.

The bottom line, though, was really quite simple. I was faced with my first real losing season. As a winaholic, I didn't know how to react.

I took winning to limits nobody could have imagined. I don't think there has ever been a person who took losses harder and kept them inside longer than I did. I crossed all boundaries of reality.

I even took it one step further. I actually believed Sparky Anderson was put on this earth solely to win.

Sparky couldn't lose. That was for the other guys.

I got fooled. I can get beat.

What Sparky must do is work hard every single day to make sure his team is prepared to win each time it takes the field. It might not win. But at least Sparky and his team are prepared with their best.

The trick now is to realize that after giving your best, there's nothing more to give. There's no shame in losing as long as you gave it your best. Win or lose, the game is finished. It's over. It's time to forget and prepare for the next one.

I work on that every day. But only one day at a time.

Vince Lombardi said, "Winning isn't everything . . . it's the only thing."

2

Winning

Vince Lombardi had a clever mind. I never was so profound. But I did believe after every loss a part of my body was supposed to die. I actually believed each loss was an insult. It was an insult to me, the team, the organization, and all of the fans. The shame that went with a loss was supposed to be felt for a long, long time.

That's the way I was raised. That's the way I played every game. It's the same way I managed. After twenty years in the major leagues, I finally learned the truth.

Winning was an obsession with me even when I was a kid. I was a kid who really didn't have a lot of physical talent.

I was a little kid always playing against guys twice my size. There were better hitters, better fielders. Guys could throw the ball twice as hard as I could. Almost everybody could beat me in a race.

I had something no one else did, though. I loved playing more than anyone in the world. Going head-to-head against anyone in anything actually made my body sizzle with excitement. I didn't have the talent they did, but I was determined not to get beat. If I couldn't do it with talent, I'd do it with will. I might get tired, but I pushed myself till everyone else dropped.

I loved to compete. Other guys had more talent. I accepted that. But I promised myself no one would outhustle me. No one was going to try harder to win than me. I was ready to bleed.

In high school basketball I was kicked out of game after game for running around like a madman. I blasted people into kingdom come. If we were down in a game, I'd knock someone into the seats. Once I knocked a guy through two doors at the end of the gym after he sank a lay-up.

On the baseball field I was exactly the same. When I went into a base, the fielder knew I was coming. If a runner was coming into second, he better get down or he'd wind up with stitch marks on his head.

I never cared how we won. I only cared that we won. If I got three hits and we lost, I was looking to punch out the biggest guy

I could find. If I went hitless and we won, I was happier than a clown at a carnival.

I took tremendous pride in driving myself. I think that's what made me a successful manager. I competed with my players. I never allowed them to work harder than me. I dared them to keep up with me. Without that drive and without burning every ounce of energy I had in me, I don't believe I would have accomplished what I have.

Somewhere along the way that drive got distorted. Somewhere it took a left turn.

Somebody in the Dodger organization must have liked the fire in me because I signed a professional contract after graduating from high school.

I reported to a camp that was filled with players who had more talent in one arm than I had in my whole body. So again I had to prove myself the only way I knew how. If those guys wanted to make it to the majors they were going to have to go through me. If they were ready to bleed a drop, I was ready to bleed a bucket.

For two years in the minor leagues I played for a manager named Clay Bryant. I loved this man so much because he was so intense about winning.

He was the meanest caged porcupine I had ever met in my life. We called him "Tiger Eyes." After every loss he came into the clubhouse and sat on the box that held our valuables and just stared at all of us players.

He never said a word. His eyes did all the talking. Those beady slits sliced right down to the soul. Guys would look up and actually start to shake. And old Clay Bryant never said a word.

We had a catcher named Danny Gaddis who actually thought Bryant's eyes belonged to the devil. I remember he told me one day, "That man is possessed." Gaddis was petrified of Bryant. He didn't know how to act.

I pulled Danny aside one day and asked him what the heck he was worried about.

"He ain't going to hurt you," I told Gaddis. "Let the man look.

All the man wants to do is win. He's trying to get all of us off our butts to do something about it."

I remember a day in Miami after we lost a close game. We had a rickety old clubhouse that had tile on the walls. It had a splintered wooden floor. It smelled like a dirty barnyard on a steamy August day. After a loss, it was a step away from hell.

A sportswriter walked in through the far end of the clubhouse. After the loss, Bryant got so upset he picked up an empty Coke bottle and fired it across the room. The bottle hit the wall inches in front of where the writer was walking. Glass went flying as if a bomb had just exploded.

The writer spun like a top. He dashed out of that clubhouse faster than any of us had gone into a base. I didn't want to see anybody hurt. But I started to laugh my butt off. I knew why Bryant was so upset. He had just suffered another loss and now he had to bleed.

There was another incident in 1958 after we had lost our sixth game in a row. We had started the week with a seven-game lead. Now it was sliced to one and Bryant was steaming.

We had a player named Billy Harris. He used to cock his hat so that it looked like he was staring out at the field. He was a real ladies' man and actually he was looking up into the stands for women. He just made it look like he was studying the game. It took all season, but Bryant thought he finally caught on to the trick.

There was a big, strong pitcher on our club named Bob Faust. After we lost our sixth straight game, Bryant started screaming at Faust.

"You're not fooling me, Faust," Bryant shrieked. "You don't even know the score, but you sure know where every woman sits in this stadium."

Bryant was yelling his lungs out while everyone sat around too scared to move. I was taking off my spikes and finally slammed them down.

"I'll tell you one damn thing," I screamed at Bryant. "You ain't a very smart manager if you don't know the guy who was doing all the looking. You got the wrong man, so get off of him right now."

The room became silent. Everyone expected a fight. But Bryant didn't say a word. Everyone showered and left.

Before the game the next day, Bryant called a meeting.

"Ain't this something?" Bryant started. "We've got some big old strong guys around here and it took this skinny little pup to stand up and straighten me out. Now let's all get our heads together and do something right for a change."

He was the manager and I was just some scrappy little dog trying to hang on. But that's the way I was. I was never afraid of anybody.

My playing career screeched to a halt at the ripe old age of twenty-nine. I was lucky to land a minor league managing job at a very young age. I was only thirty when I managed at Toronto in Class AAA in 1964.

The responsibility of management certainly didn't cool my hot-pepper style. I took nothing from no one. I was possessed with winning.

Most of the players on that club were older than me. Still, I was a raving maniac—I mean really wild. I went crazy over everything. I must have been thrown out of fifteen to twenty games my first year as a manager. My wife, Carol, used to say that she better get to the game for the first inning or she might not see her husband in uniform.

I remember going into the clubhouse one day after a tough loss. Bill Smith was our trainer and he came waltzing in after we did carrying a bagful of hamburgers. When we lost, I believed there was no time for any nonsense like eating. Everybody was supposed to keep their head down in stone dead silence and think about what had just gone wrong. A piece of everybody's body was supposed to die after a loss. It was time to bleed.

"Where in the hell do you think you are going with those hamburgers, Smitty?" I screamed at the trainer.

"One of the players wanted them," Smitty shot back.

"Well, you just walk those fine pieces of meat right over here," I told Smitty.

He handed me the bag. I walked over to the middle of the room and stood next to a trash can.

"Do these hamburgers belong to anyone in this room?" I asked sarcastically in the chilly silence.

No one said a word. No one dared to speak.

Slowly I took each burger out of the bag. One by one I squeezed them into a ball of grease before slamming them into the trash can.

When I was done I stared at every player. Then I walked into the little room that served as the manager's office. A few minutes later, a player named Lee Tate walked quietly into the room.

"Skip, I want to tell you something," Tate almost whispered to me. "Those hamburgers were mine. I really want to apologize, but my wife and kids drove all day from Buffalo to see me. They didn't have a chance to eat so I asked Smitty to buy me some burgers."

Now it was my turn to be quiet. That's something in itself. I felt so low I didn't know what to say.

"Lee, I feel so terrible," I finally managed to say. "I had no idea those were for your kids."

I yelled for Smitty.

"Go out and get me some hamburgers, Smitty. But this time, double the order."

Smitty shot back.

"For crying out loud," he said. "First you squeeze them to smithereens and now you want twice as many."

Smitty took the money and came back with more. For once in my life I kept my mouth shut the rest of the day.

There was another incident while I was with Toronto after a doubleheader in Buffalo. It was in the middle of summer. It was hotter than a Mexican pepper and we lost both games.

We walked quietly into the clubhouse after the last out. In the middle of the room was a table full of freshly sliced watermelon. It looked great. I know my players wanted to dig into it because I wanted to dig in, too.

I walked right by the table, tough, and sat in the corner pulling off my spikes. My head was down when I heard one of the guys say, "Ah . . . this tastes great."

My head shot up like there was a spring on my neck. The first person I saw was Lee Tate. I'm not sure he had even touched a slice. I jumped out of my chair and darted across the room.

"So this is good, right Mr. Tate?" I shouted.

Then I proceeded to throw every piece of watermelon all over the room. A few slices stuck to the wall. A couple hung from the ceiling. Eventually all of it wound up melting on the floor in a red sea that looked like someone had slashed his wrists.

After I finally calmed down, I asked where the clubhouse man was. He was an old man. They told me he was downstairs where he lived, crying like a baby.

Now I felt about three feet tall. Sparky had done it again. I went downstairs to apologize to the old man.

He was so upset, he was almost sick. I told him I was sorry and that I would take care of everything. I went back upstairs and waited till everybody left. I found a bucket, a mop, and some old rags. I polished every inch of that place. Every time I eat a piece of watermelon now I remember my little spectacle.

I went from watermelons to television sets. One time after a loss I actually picked up a TV set and was ready to heave it across the room till some of the guys grabbed me and took it out of my hands.

My all-timer in the minor leagues, though, came in 1965 when I managed for Rock Hill in the St. Louis Cardinals' organization. I didn't know Rock Hill from diddly-doo. But it was the only job I could get. We had the absolute worst players in professional ball.

I got into an argument with an umpire at home plate. I have no idea what the argument was about, but I know it got heated and he accidentally bumped me.

When he bumped me, I went berserk. I grabbed him right around the top of the throat with both hands. When I let go, I grabbed his tie and tried to throw him as far as I could.

After letting him go again, I realized I was done. Not just for the game. For my entire career. A manager doesn't attack an umpire like that without getting kicked out of the game for life.

When the game was over, I went in to pack my bags. I thought I was packing them for the last time. My baseball career was history.

There was a knock on the door. When I opened it, that umpire stood there calmly and said he wanted to explain something.

"You know I bumped you first," he said. "I want you to know that I don't have anything to say to the league about it if you don't."

I don't recall that man's name. But I never will forget him. I looked him right in the eye.

"Can I kiss you right here?" I said to him.

Not a word was mentioned by him or me. That's the last time I ever grabbed an umpire. I'll never forget I could have been barred from baseball for life.

When I got to the major leagues I still was a raving maniac. My first few years in Cincinnati I was a holy terror.

I used to have team meetings in Cincinnati where I'd throw everything in sight. Trash cans and food wound up all over the place.

I was in trouble with the umpires all the time. One day in Los Angeles I raced out to argue with Doug Harvey at first base.

"When I get done talking to you, Mr. Harvey, you're going to run me out of this game," I shouted.

He looked at me calmly.

"No I'm not, Mr. Anderson," he said. "I'm going to run you right now."

"Wait a minute," I said. "Don't I even get a chance to talk?"

"You told me that when you were done I was going to run you," he said. "There's no sense even listening so please get out of the park right now."

To this day, Doug and I joke about that incident.

My last three years in the National League I finally grew up and became a gentleman. Some of those umpires still can't believe the way I've changed.

I finally realized that umpires are not out there to cause trouble for you. They have a job to do and they can make mistakes. They're human. They're no different than any of us.

An umpire now has to make a blatant mistake for me to rip him. If I think something is wrong, I go out to tell him. But I do it very civilly. I do not use obscenities. I tell him I think he blew the call and the reason why. Then that's the end of it. There's nothing more to say.

I am twenty times calmer now than I was in my first year as a pro in 1953. When I was young I used to have arguments when I honestly thought I was having a heart attack. I got so worked up I couldn't breathe. I couldn't lift my arms up. They got so heavy I had to keep them at my side.

Now I never get like that. For the last fifteen years I have learned to keep everything inside. Maybe that was part of the problem. I don't know. When I was younger I was able to take it. When I got older all that pressure got cramped up. After every loss I felt rats gnawing at my stomach.

Losing never became easier to take. I just learned not to show it.

Even during the good years a loss was like swallowing poison. Every loss sliced a little piece of my innards. It felt like a four-sided razor blade inside my body. It started to twist and turn from the top of my throat and work its way slowly down to the pit of my stomach.

I bled. I cried. But I kept it all inside so no one could see. After each loss I sat quietly with the writers. I answered all their questions. I never raised my voice.

No one knew what was happening inside of me. Sitting there calmly while my insides were dripping down to the floor had to be my greatest piece of acting.

I preached to the players and also the writers: "There's nothing so important about winning in baseball that it should affect your health or your family. No matter what happens tonight, the sun will shine tomorrow. And if it isn't shining, it will either be raining or snowing. But that's the worst that can happen."

I tried to follow my own advice. I even pretended to show that I did. But I was a hypocrite. I preached all the right stuff, but I never practiced what I preached. I knew all the right words, but I never listened to them.

I always looked at losing as a personal failure. Losing, to me, was embarrassment. I always felt like I had let people down. I felt like I was less of a man. There was dishonor in losing. And I felt like it was all my fault.

After a loss on the road, I was embarrassed to walk through the lobby of the hotel. I actually felt like people looked at me strangely. I felt like I was wearing a scarlet letter. It was a giant L.

After a loss at home I felt embarrassed from the time I drove into the parking lot till it was time to start the next game. I felt like I had let everyone down—everyone who worked there and all the fans who had come to the game.

If I had scheduled an engagement for after a game, I wouldn't go if we lost. To this day I'm still sorry for the way I acted when I managed at Cincinnati and we lost to the Dodgers in Los Angeles.

My father loved baseball. He lived in Los Angeles and couldn't wait until the Reds came to town. He was so proud to go to Dodger Stadium to watch his son manage the Big Red Machine.

The Big Red Machine, though, better have won the ball game. Because when we lost, I never stuck around. Not even to talk to my folks. They knew I didn't want to talk to anyone so they'd leave right away.

How sad is that? My dad died on May 17, 1984. I still carry the guilt for having acted as I did.

That's the way I took winning and losing. I took losing to limits no one even knew existed. They were dangerous. Eventually I crossed the line.

11

My first nineteen years in the big leagues I had only one team that finished under .500. That was the 1971 Reds, and they were only four under.

I've been really lucky. I've been blessed. I've managed in five World Series and won three of them. I've managed in seven League Championship Series and won five of them.

Sometimes I wonder if all that success was a blessing or a curse. Certainly I'm grateful for all my good fortune. But it got me to believing that Sparky was supposed to win.

Carol knows me better than any person in the world. She warned me about my obsession. She tried to help me before it got out of control.

"What are you going to do if you have a club that simply can't win?" she used to ask. "What happens the day you wind up with a club that plays hard but simply isn't good enough to win?"

I didn't believe it could happen. But that day finally arrived.

It was May 19, 1989. That was the day I admitted I was a winaholic. That became the first day of my new life.

Going Home

Did you ever have that dream where you walk into a room filled with your friends only to realize that you're standing there buck naked? You want to crawl into a hole and never show your face. The embarrassment is overwhelming. The shame gushes throughout your body, even into your teeth.

That's the closest I can come to describing the way I felt my first few days home in Thousand Oaks.

Here we were in the middle of the season. My team was playing every day. It battled. It was struggling like a plow horse in a race for three-year-olds, but it wasn't giving up.

Meanwhile I was two thousand miles away. At home . . . with nothing to do with my club.

That's when it hit me. I was embarrassed. I was ashamed. It was almost impossible to accept the fact that I was actually at home in the middle of a season.

I kept thinking it was all a dream. This couldn't happen to Sparky. It happened, all right. It was as real as the fact that I had left my club in last place.

I felt I had let my club down. I felt I had betrayed so many friends. I felt like I would never be able to face anyone again. For the first few days back, I thought I'd never be able to manage again. Twenty years in the big leagues and suddenly it was over. Sparky didn't end with a flash. He ended with a whimper.

I tried to figure out where it all started. How did it ever get to this?

I knew I always took winning to extremes. But nightmares like this aren't supposed to be real. Even while we were struggling, I tried to keep up my superman act. I made every appearance. I returned every phone call from the media. I kept up my visits to the kids in the hospitals.

Meanwhile my team was scuffling and there was absolutely nothing I could do.

I was powerless. I had no magic tricks.

We were losing games and losing players. We had so many players hurt, we started to look like a hospital ward.

I guess it started to peak the first week of May. Injuries ambushed our players like the Indians wiped out Custer. It seemed like every day when we got to the park, somebody else would come up hurt. Somebody had a bad arm. Someone else had a twisted knee. Someone had a stiff back. The topper came when Jack Morris went down.

Morris came up with a bad right elbow and that hurt me more than any of the others. I know what a competitor Jack Morris is. I was with him for ten years and only twice did he not take the ball. Once was when his arm swelled up from getting hit by a ball in practice. The other time he had a tender elbow and I made

14

him skip a turn. He wanted to pitch, but I wouldn't let him. Now he was struggling, too.

My mind was racing for ways to put this together. I juggled lineups in my mind and thought about switching players here and there. I went to the park earlier each day. I fooled with different combinations. I tried different things. Just when I thought I had something, another player would go down.

My mind was spinning constantly. There never was a break. Even when I slept there was no let up at all.

Two nights in a row I slept for eight hours. That's more than I get in a normal night's sleep, but when I woke up, it was like I hadn't slept at all. I wrestled with my mind even in my sleep. I kept fighting with something over which I had no control. When I finally would pass out, my sleep was filled with nightmares. These weren't your average horror stories. These babies were straight out of Stephen King.

I remember one nightmare as clear as day. I was sitting in my office in the clubhouse when our trainer walked in.

"What's the new problem today?" I asked him. "Who did we lose now?"

I remember him looking at me and breaking into a sheepish smile.

"Well . . ." he answered. Then suddenly I woke up.

In another one I walked into the clubhouse and a few players were there even earlier than me.

In one corner was Fred Lynn wrapped all over like a mummy. Alan Trammell had his back wrapped so tightly he couldn't even breathe. And Jeff Robinson had his elbow wrapped so that it wouldn't fall off his arm.

I'd wake from these dreams sweating like a lawn sprinkler. My body actually ached from the torture during the night.

There's no excuse for taking anything that hard. But my mind and body kept doing it. They were both racing out of control.

I think it came to a head on May 11 when we played an exhibition game with our AAA club at Toledo. Our general manager, Bill Lajoie, had to call up three minor league pitchers to pitch for us because so many of ours were hurt.

In fact, we had so many guys hurting that I became quite concerned we couldn't give the people a show. That hit me like a low blow. When hardworking people pay good money to see a game with the big league club, they deserve a show. I knew we weren't prepared to give one.

I did three or four TV shows with the local stations. An exhibition game with the major league team is a big date for a AAA club. It generates a lot of money and often makes the difference for the year.

After I finished the interviews I walked down the left field line. I spotted a wooden structure and stood up on it to sign autographs for the fans.

I stood there and signed for about forty-five minutes. I had a bad feeling about the game coming up and felt these people deserved something.

When I finished I walked across the field to the first base side. There was Alan Trammell doing the same thing I had done. He was suffering from a bad back and wasn't able to play. I don't know if Alan was thinking the same thing I was, but I sure was proud of him.

I walked right up next to him and signed for another half hour. All the time I kept thinking that what we were about to give the fans wasn't right. I hoped we could satisfy them this way.

Once the game started, my Stephen King nightmares became real. We looked like we were playing in quicksand. We were going down to a slow painful death.

Toledo had been hit with a rash of doubleheaders. Manager John Wockenfuss was forced to pitch in order to keep his staff intact.

I don't blame John. But I knew what was going to happen.

When something like that happens, the game turns into a joke. No one bears down. Players go to the plate swinging just to get out of there.

Sure enough it happened. John set us down without a run for five innings.

It gave the media a chance to say we couldn't even beat a minor league club. It also was the start of the longest week of my life.

After the game, we bussed to Cleveland for a weekend series. I'll never forget the first night there. As soon as we arrived, I tried to go to sleep. I figured the best way to get through the night was not to think about anything at all.

Good idea . . . bad results.

I woke up in the middle of the night. I was sweating so hard it was like I had just come in from the rain. I got out of bed and sat in a lounge chair. I kept thinking to myself, "Have we gotten this bad?"

We beat the Indians the first game. Then they bounced back to whip us the next two.

The bus ride back to Detroit was the longest trip of my life. Interstate 75 at night isn't exactly a picture. But I could have been on another planet for all I knew. I remember sitting there, just staring into space. I didn't say much. I couldn't if I had to. I just kept wondering what was going to happen next.

We came back to a three-game series against the White Sox. Fortunately for us, they were having problems, too.

We won the first two games and finished the series on Wednesday. It turned into one of the most frustrating games of my whole career.

We took a 7–5 lead into the top of the ninth inning. Willie Hernandez was pitching and got their first batter out. Then it all happened. They proceeded to put men on base as if it were a parade.

When it was all over, the White Sox had scored five runs. They took a 10–7 lead into the last of the ninth and quickly shut us down.

It was just one more loss. But it was the method more than the result that hurt. To make things worse, Thursday was an off-day. There's nothing worse in baseball than a day off after a fiasco like that. The best thing is to play a game to get the poison out of your system. This time the sore festered. It got uglier and uglier.

I sat around the house all day. I couldn't push myself to do anything. All I did was think. I thought about all the things that were going wrong and what I could possibly do to stop them.

That was the problem. I was powerless.

That evening disaster struck. I'll never forget it as long as I live.

I attended a charity function to raise money for Children's Hospital. It was a fancy affair where guests paid to play that game where someone draws a picture and the rest of the team tries to guess what it is.

The game wasn't that bad. All the schmoozing that surrounded it was murder. I was introduced to all these people. I had to shake hands, smile, and pretend I was the happiest person on the face of the earth.

I had to be Sparky Anderson. At the time, I never wanted to see Sparky again.

Each minute was an hour. I felt like my skin was going to fall off. I was afraid my bones were going to crumble to the floor. I really had no idea what I was doing. I just kept smiling and tried to talk as little as I could. They were the longest three hours of my entire life.

I'm not sure how I ever drove home. It's a miracle I kept the car on the road. I remember getting home about ten-thirty. I was too tired to walk upstairs to the bedroom. I plopped into a chair and just sat there and sweat.

When I finally did go upstairs, I collapsed into bed. I guess I fell asleep. But it sure wasn't peaceful.

The next morning our president, Jim Campbell, called. Later he had our team physician, Dr. Clarence Livingood, call. Just from my voice they knew something was wrong.

The press release explaining my departure said I was exhausted. That's 100 percent correct. But I was not only physically exhausted. I was mentally burned out.

I no longer could do all the things that used to come so easily.

I no longer could be everything that everyone else wanted me to be.

I no longer could be Sparky Anderson. More important, I had no desire to be.

They convinced me that I needed time off. They told me to go home to Thousand Oaks to regain my strength and get recharged.

Sparky would have fought the mere suggestion of going home. This time there was no fight. Sparky was whipped. There was no alternative.

So on the morning of May 19 with the Kansas City Royals in town, I packed my bags to return to Thousand Oaks, thinking I had worn a major league uniform for the last time in my life.

I remember three suitcases sitting in the middle of my bedroom. I remember sweeping through all my drawers and simply dumping things into the bags. I remember walking into my closet and raking all my suits together. I kept one out and stuffed the rest into the bags.

There was a drizzle on the way to the airport. All I kept thinking about were the good times I had enjoyed in Detroit.

Billy Consolo is one of our coaches. We've been friends since high school. He lives with Carol and me during the season. He accompanied me home. But I'm sure he never realized I was thinking I would never return.

On the plane I remember being as calm as could be. I sat there talking to Billy. Some people asked for autographs. One person asked what I was doing on the plane when we had a game that night.

I told him that a personal emergency had come up at home. At least I was smart enough to think of that. It was true. No one suspected the emergency was me.

I remember Billy saying to me, "Do you want to turn this plane around and go back? You seem to be all right."

I just smiled and tried to relax as best as I could. I counted the minutes till we finally landed.

When we got off the plane, Carol was waiting at the gate. Carol has always been my best friend. I don't say this because we've been married for thirty-seven years, I say it because it's true. She understands me more than anyone. I know I can depend on her.

Carol has learned to tolerate Sparky. She even has come to appreciate him. But she loves George. And I'm not ashamed to say I love her.

So when I saw her, I honestly felt relaxed. Finally there was a sense of protection. No one could get to me now.

Carol and I went to the car as Billy collected the baggage. Then it was home to Thousand Oaks for my first "vacation" ever in the middle of a season.

When I got home I was hungry. I made myself a sandwich and sank into my favorite chair.

I called all my kids to let them know I was fine. I didn't want them hearing anything first on the news or reading it in the paper. I called my mom and told her not to worry. Then I turned on the radio to catch the Tiger score.

"I can't believe you," Carol said. "You just come home and the first thing you want to do is find out the score."

She didn't have to worry about me listening to anything after that. The first night back I slept for sixteen hours. There were no dreams. I was dead till the next day.

The first thing I did after I awoke was to go downstairs and slump into an easy chair. After resting there for a while, I went back to bed. I slept for another twelve hours.

The first five days home I never stepped outside. Except for my kids, Carol let no one in. She not only didn't let anyone inside the house, but no one got through to me on the telephone. The president of the United States would have had a tough time.

Carol fielded all calls. She protected me like a baby. She kept a log of all the calls. When she was done, it looked like the Los Angeles yellow pages.

I can't even recall all the calls I received. It seemed like the phone never stopped ringing. Roger Craig called a couple of times. There were calls from Chuck Daly, Tom Lasorda, Johnny Bench, Vin Scully, Tony LaRussa, Dick Williams, Chuck Tanner, and a lot of other sports figures.

After a few days home I started to receive gifts. I got more flowers than someone in a funeral home.

The cards and letters were overwhelming. Our mailman told us he'd never worked so hard. They came from people all over the United States, not just from Detroit or Cincinnati. I got some from Montana, Virginia, and Oregon. You name a state and I got at least one card from there.

Carol let me read them till I'd start to get emotional. Then she'd take them away.

The one I remember most came from Mickey Cobb, the Kansas City Royals' trainer. Mickey has a handicap and is one of the hardest workers I've ever seen in the game. His note said that I was special because I always step back to acknowledge him even when I'm surrounded by a horde of reporters. He said that makes him feel important. It means more to him than anything that's ever happened to him.

That's when I became most emotional and Carol put a stop to the cards.

I told Carol that at least I learned something. I must not have done too many wrong things to people if everybody remembered me this way. That was a tremendous feeling. Not the fact that people worried about me, but the fact that I must have done a few things right to make people feel good. That really gave me a lift.

After a couple of days home, my good friend George McCarthy came by. George is a treasure. He's over eighty years old and one of the wisest men I've been fortunate to meet. We play golf every single day during the winter.

George didn't want to bring him, but another friend tagged along. George knew that Carol wouldn't let the two of them come inside.

"The gestapo stopped me at the door," Georgie told me later.

A few days later George called on the phone. I told Carol I wanted to talk to him.

"When I'm ready, I'll call you," I told George. He knew what I meant. He was wise enough to let me be.

On the fifth day of being inside, I finally ventured across the street to see my neighbors. I had nothing important to say. I just wanted to talk. I told them the truth. I told them exactly how I felt. I didn't want to see my other friends, though, because I still felt embarrassed.

Here it was in the middle of the season and I was at home doing absolutely nothing. It was a brand new feeling. I didn't know what to think. It felt so strange to be sitting in my house when I knew I was supposed to be at work trying to help my club.

I thought people would look at me as if I were some kind of a freak. I thought people would think I was crazy.

But it turned out to be just the opposite. I learned that people really understand that things like this happen. I learned that human beings can take just so much. Some can take more than others. But everyone has a limit. People understand.

It can happen to a mother, to a father, to a sister, to a son.

This time it happened to Sparky Anderson. Sparky has his limits, too.

So after five days of doing nothing, I decided to visit some friends. I simply said "the hell with it." I went to the coffee shop where I normally meet my friends in the winter.

Then I called Georgie with a two-word message: "I'm ready."

The next day he came by alone and we went out to hit golf balls. I was nervous. But I knew I had to try.

The first few days we never kept score. We just hit the ball and enjoyed being on the course. I started with about three dozen balls. After the first couple of days I was down to about six. I was hitting the balls all over the place. I lost them in the woods, in the water, and down the canyon that the rattlesnakes call home. I'm a bad golfer to begin with, but my concentration just wasn't there. My mind wandered. So did the golf balls.

After a couple of days, we kept score. I noticed my concentration coming back. The proof was in my golf bag. In two days I lost only two balls.

I also noticed I became more interested in getting all of the baseball scores. I wanted to get them as soon as I could. I turned on the radio a couple of minutes before all the scores were read every half hour.

After about ten days at home, I told Carol I was getting ready to go back. All my physical tests had checked out perfectly. The doctor told me he wished he could be as healthy as I was when he reached fifty-five.

Dr. Livingood suggested that I return on June 19 when the team was in Oakland.

"It won't be June 19," I told Dr. Livingood. "If I'm ready to go, then I'm going back sooner. If I can't handle it then, then I know that I'm done. Either I'm ready or I can't take it anymore."

I figured if I felt healthy, then I had an obligation to return to work. Jim Campbell and the Detroit Baseball Club have treated me better than any manager in history.

I remember Jim's words when I left:

"You are going to determine when you come back. Nobody else. I don't want you to feel any pressure to return. When you feel ready, then you come back. There's no pressure. I want you healthy even if it takes the whole year."

How can anyone be treated better than that? That's like giving someone a license to steal. I never stole anything in my life. I wasn't about to start now.

I felt strong and sharp. I said to myself, "If I feel this good and then can't handle it, then that means I'm done. That means my nerves are shot."

Jumbled nerves such as I had don't come up overnight. They come from twenty years in the dugout worrying about every little play and player. They come from twenty years of eighth and ninth innings and second-guessing every move I've made. They come from going into my office after every game and having to put down my cup because my hand was jumping so much I couldn't even catch the coffee in the cup.

I actually thought that was wonderful. I thought it was part of the excitement of the game. That was the thrill. That was my lifeline.

But it had taken its toll. And it demanded a terrific price. It was eating my body up. The doctor told me I was healthy in every organ they tested. But I was stressed out. He said the best medicine would be to walk away.

I just couldn't do it. I wanted to be in the dugout. I made a promise to myself, though, that I would not cheat the Detroit Baseball Club. They had been too good to me for me to take money under false pretenses.

I promised myself and Carol that if I could not take the losses along with the wins and all the daily stuff that goes with it, I would walk away. She convinced me that I could walk with my head held high. I've climbed mountains most men only dream about. There is no reason to walk with my head hung low.

I also promised myself that Sparky had been in control long enough. Now it was time for George to take over. It was time to be myself.

All she asked was for me to give each day a chance. If a bad day comes along, just battle the day. A bad day lasts only twenty-four hours. If you can get through that bad one, a good day might follow.

She convinced me not to make any spur-of-the-moment decisions. Take each day one at a time. Then leave it for what it is.

I gave my word. Then we checked the schedule to see what the best date would be for my return.

I had been advised that if I returned on June 19, the team would be in Oakland and I could avoid some of the media crunch. All the doctors and club executives were only looking out for my good. But I wanted to return with the team in Detroit. That's where I left. That's where I had to return.

The Detroit media had been extremely cooperative by not bothering me while I had been at home. I didn't think it was fair to return on the road and give the out-of-town writers the first shot.

24

Boston was in Detroit on June 4. I checked the papers and noticed that Roger Clemens was scheduled to pitch.

That was the clincher. June 4 would be the day. I wanted to show everybody I wasn't afraid to face the war. Carol arranged for the airline ticket and I was ready to make my way back. It was a five-hour flight. But I knew my return would take much longer than that.

It might take a year. It might take longer. But I promised myself to deal with it one day at a time.

I was far more nervous returning to Detroit than I was going home. But I knew it had to be done. And I was going to face it head on. I had to find out if I could still do it. I had to find out if Sparky would finally listen to George.

Coming Back

It was Sunday, June 3. I was getting ready for my trip back to Detroit.

I went to church in the morning and said a couple of extra prayers. I wanted things to go just right. This time Sparky knew he needed help, and this time he wasn't too proud to ask.

I won't lie; I was totally scared. Going back to Detroit made me a lot more nervous than when I had left. When I left I was in such a state of shock, I really didn't grasp what the heck was happening.

When I came home I was quite emotional. Bizarre thoughts ran wild through my mind. I kept thinking my career had ended. I was nakedly ashamed that I had to leave my team in the middle of a season.

So I really didn't have the chance to feel nervous about anything. I thought my fate had been sealed. I just wanted to get back home.

Returning was quite a different story. I didn't know what to expect. I felt like an insect. I was going under the microscope like some bug in a biology class.

I wondered what all the people were thinking. I tried to anticipate what all the questions would be. I kept running the questions through my mind and answering them at the same time.

"What were your thoughts when you first went home?" "How does it feel to be back in Detroit?" "What did you learn from your seventeen days away?"

Then I started having questions of my own. Do I walk back in with my head held high? Or do I slip around the corner and just try to blend back into the scene?

Finally I said enough was enough. Here I've been in this game for twenty years. I've been to the top of the mountain several times. Why should I go back with my head down when some guys who hadn't even been around three years had theirs in the clouds?

I had to show everybody that Sparky was back. But I had to show them that George was in control.

Nevertheless, I was still nervous.

The day I left Thousand Oaks, Carol wouldn't let me be by myself. We drove to the Los Angeles airport. She waited at the gate till the plane took off.

Carol wanted to return to Detroit with me. But our daughter had recently had another baby. Carol had her hands full trying to help her out.

When the plane took off I felt a suffocating sense of being alone. I distinctly remember saying to myself, "Oh my God . . . here we go again."

Two days from then the Los Angeles Lakers were going to start the NBA finals at Detroit so there seemed to be a lot of Detroiters going back for the playoffs.

Several people recognized me and asked how I felt. I told them I was fine. That was the truth. But no one could have imagined all the thoughts racing through my mind.

I wasn't nervous about returning to the dugout. I was worried about the press conference scheduled for the next day. That was going to be really tough. There was no way around it.

We tried to keep my return as quiet as possible. I wasn't sure if the writers would pick up on what flight I was on. There was no commotion, though. I slipped back in as quietly as I had slipped out.

If there had been a group of reporters waiting at the airport, I wouldn't have said a thing. I had made up my mind to say everything at the press conference. I wanted to be fair to everyone because everyone had been fair to me by not calling.

A friend met me at the airport at about eight-thirty that night. Except for some "welcome backs" from people in the terminal, I was able to get to the car without any sort of commotion.

I have walked through that terminal so many times over the last ten years that I recognize a lot of the skycaps and other people that work there. They were all so friendly. They showed genuine concern. Still, I felt so alone. I felt I was walking through that airport for the first time in my life.

We took the same route back to my condo that we had taken seventeen days before. The same roads as when I left for Thousand Oaks and thought I'd never see them again.

But there I was, back to take over as manager of the Tigers. There I was trying to find out if I could take the pressures of the dugout again.

Even the condo seemed strange. I had lived in it for ten years, but suddenly it felt more like a hotel than home. I woke up once in the middle of the night. In spite of the three-hour time difference, though, I was able to slip back to sleep almost as easily as I woke.

I got up at about seven-thirty and went downstairs for a cup of coffee. I was already edgy because I knew that clock was going to keep ticking. Each tick brought that press conference a little bit closer.

It's a thirty-five-minute drive from my condo to the ball park. I left at one o'clock and knew exactly when I'd arrive by the landmarks I've set in my mind. When I drove by Henry Ford Hospital my heart really started to pound. In just five minutes, I'd be back at the park.

I'll never forget the feeling I had when I turned off the freeway onto the Trumbull exit. I drove up the ramp and the ballpark stared at me.

"Oh my God, there it is!" I actually said that out loud and I was the only person in the car. My hands got cold. I was tempted to turn around. Suddenly playing golf in Thousand Oaks didn't seem like such a bad deal.

Driving through the parking-lot gate I got more nervous than I thought I ever could be. It was a great feeling to be back, but I was really edgy. I had been driving into this lot for the last ten years. Now I felt like a stranger. I knew I was supposed to be there, but I wondered what right I had to drive into the parking lot at Tiger Stadium.

I went upstairs to visit Jim Campbell and Bill Lajoie. Then I visited all the offices to say hello to all the secretaries and workers. Every day when we're at home I try to say hello to everyone. This time I didn't know what to expect. I didn't know if they would welcome me back or look at me like I was some kind of freak.

Everyone was so cheerful. Everyone seemed to be so glad I was back. These were people I had known for ten years, nevertheless, I felt as if I were meeting them for the very first time.

The press conference was scheduled for 3:00. I rehearsed in my mind exactly what I wanted to say.

I made up my mind to tell nothing but the truth. I went home because of exhaustion. But the exhaustion was more than physical. It also was mental and I wasn't ashamed to admit it.

Some of the media felt I was subdued. They should have. If they couldn't tell that, then they were lousy reporters.

Of course I was subdued! That press conference was the scariest thing I ever had to do. Over the years I've faced millions of cameras and answered more questions than most reporters ever will ask in a career. But never before had I ever had to face a roomful of reporters to talk about myself. I bared my soul because I knew it had to be done.

I was subdued because I wanted them to know exactly how I felt. If I had been joking and kidding, then I wouldn't have been able to explain the pain I went through.

This was serious stuff. I had left my ball club in the middle of the season. It wasn't the time for wisecracks and jokes. I don't believe all of them understood that.

"The word *exhausted* means you're very tired," I told them at the press conference. "I was not only exhausted, I was mentally exhausted. I had taken all of this so hard inside of me that it had worked my body up. I worked my body up so hard to the point at which I couldn't take it anymore. My hand was shaking. I knew something was very wrong. I found out from all this that I could not have gone another day. Not one more day."

I think I surprised a few people. I don't think they expected to hear some of the things I said. But I had to face it straight up. I had to look the monster dead in the eye and dare it to bring me down.

I did one other thing at the press conference that made me feel proud. While I was gone an article had appeared in a Detroit paper that said one of the reasons I had gone home was because Tom Monaghan and I had exchanged angry words over the team he had given me.

The story was absolutely false and I made sure that everyone there heard it from me. I read that story while I was at home and it bothered me a lot. It bothered me because Tom Monaghan is such a decent human being. He should not be subjected to lies like that.

31

I don't know how long I will manage in Detroit. Nobody knows. But I have told every young manager that comes into the league the same thing. When I quit managing in Detroit, if you're asked to replace me, don't turn the opportunity down. You'll never get an opportunity to manage in a better place because of the Tiger ownership, its president, and its general manager.

Before taking the job in 1979, I asked Ralph Houk about the Tigers. Ralph managed there before me for five years. He told me those very words and I never forgot them. That's basically why I chose Detroit over several other teams. Those words are as true today as they were when I first went to Detroit.

I had nine wonderful years in Cincinnati. I'll never forget those players. But never have I been treated as I have been by Tom Monaghan, Jim Campbell, and Bill Lajoie. They are professionals. They are friends.

In all my years with the Tigers, I have never been told what to do. So any mistakes that were made were made by me. Never have I been treated so well, and if I ever go to another club, I will never be treated as well. Tom Monaghan has probably never raised his voice to another person. So it bothered me quite a bit to think someone would write that he and I had had words.

What I didn't tell them at the press conference was that Tom did give me a call. He told me he wanted me to be his manager until I was in my rocking chair. That was as big a lift as I ever could have expected.

When the press conference ended I went back to my office. I called Carol to tell her it was over. I still was nervous. But it was a good nervous. It was the kind you feel after doing something good.

Players stopped by as they came in the clubhouse. Some were surprised to see me. Some didn't know I was back. Frank Tanana asked why I didn't call a team meeting. I told him I thought I might have gotten emotional. I preferred to meet all the guys one by one.

The pregame activities were as hectic as ever. Each TV station wanted a separate interview. Each writer wanted the same. I knew what to expect, though. I was prepared.

I kept waiting for the game to start. I wanted the whole thing to be over.

When I took the lineup card to home plate, I didn't know what to expect. I didn't know if the crowd was going to cheer or boo. My legs were like jelly. I remember telling the umpires, "I have no idea what's going to happen."

I felt good when I reached home plate. The crowd was cheering. I could hear some fans sitting near home plate when they started to chant: "Welcome home, Sparky."

People are generally kind. They're sensitive to problems because they have them, too. Even when they boo, they're not booing the person. They're just frustrated because they love their team so much.

In the dugout, I still didn't feel right. This was the same dugout that was home for ten years. This was the same dugout I was standing in when we won a World Series. I've managed more major league games in that dugout than in any other in the United States.

Nevertheless, I felt like a stranger. I felt like a stranger till I made my first pitching move. That's also an experience I'll never forget.

My legs still felt like rubber when I jumped onto the field. I always keep my head down when I walk to the mound to remove a pitcher. Only this time I honestly wasn't sure if I was headed in the right direction. I didn't know if I was headed toward the mound or if, by mistake, I had zigged a little in the wrong direction. Suddenly it rushed through my mind that I might be walking the wrong way.

I knew I was on the infield grass. I took a peek down and saw I was off a little to the left. I had to zero back in to the right to make it to the mound. All I needed was to wind up at second base to make a pitching change. People might have thought I was a little crazy before. Now they would think I really had cracked.

After that first move, I felt I had really gotten back into the swing of the game. I thought I managed as well as I possibly could. We still lost the game, 5–2.

I felt I was able to keep us in the game, though. I felt my moves gave us a chance to win. I did my best and there was nothing else I could have done.

After the game I was relieved it was over. But I stayed on guard for the postgame interviews. I knew someone was going to try to snipe. I was prepared for some cutie pie to say something smart.

Normally after a loss I keep my head down while the reporters ask questions. It's a habit I've followed all my life. That night, however, I made sure to change my routine. I kept my head up high and answered all questions. I looked each man in the eye and didn't dodge a one. I knew if my head was down they'd make something of it.

It also taught me a lesson. It helped me to remember what I must practice the rest of my career. Prepare my team to the best of its ability. Then let the players play and forget about the rest. I cannot control the destiny of a game. I can only prepare my team and then let it happen. When it's over, it's over. Now get your team ready for the next day.

So the first day was history. And quite a day it was. I did make it through, though. That's all that mattered.

The next night we beat Boston. And I was able to handle that, too. It used to be after a win I thought my team could never lose. Not this time. I reminded myself it was just one more day.

That's the way I handled all the games the rest of the season. Win or lose, I let them go once they were over. That's the way I must handle all of them the rest of my career.

No one win is going to make a team for a whole season. No one loss is going to destroy it for a year.

More important than that—no number of wins or losses, no matter how many, ever can total enough to ruin a person's life.

Losing isn't easier to accept now. It never was easy and I don't think it ever will be. Losing shouldn't be easy to accept. But losing, in itself, shouldn't be the yardstick of success. How we go about it is what counts. What kind of person we become from it is the true measure.

I accept losses in a different way now. I am no longer embarrassed by them. I no longer feel insulted or that I let anyone down. Not as long as I've prepared my team to perform at its highest level. Once I've done that, there's nothing else I can do.

I cannot get rid of the hurt from losing. I don't want to. If I ever lose that, then I lose my competitive edge. If that ever goes then I've lost my purpose. But after the last out of every loss I must accept that there'll be a tomorrow. In fact, it's more than there'll be a tomorrow; it's that I want there to be a tomorrow. That's the big difference: I want tomorrow to come.

Throughout my career I took for granted there'd always be tomorrow. After being out of the game even for a short time, I realized there might not be a tomorrow.

I don't suggest people go away to get their minds going in the right direction. I took it to extremes. I did it as only Sparky could.

After ten years in baseball, though, a manager should stay out for a month and see how much he loves the game. I found out in just seventeen days that baseball is a marvelous game. It's marvelous even in losing.

In losing you discover how people can perform. You find out the people who don't want to perform. When things go bad there are some guys who don't want to perform. They can't rise up. They want to wrap it up. They want it nice all the time.

That's the way I always had it. I had nineteen years of everything being nice. I was spoiled. I was spoiled beyond rotten.

Now I have to work. It doesn't make losing feel any less painful at all. But I accept the losses for what they are. I never want those tomorrows to stop coming.

I always used to say that the day would come when I'd have to pay back all the good things that have happened to me in baseball. I might have to pay back double. But at least now I know how to do it. At least now I have the opportunity.

I don't claim to be a religious person. But I know God never promised us happiness. All He promised was the opportunity to achieve happiness. The rest is up to us. That's the promise of tomorrow.

Being sent home in the middle of the season was, at the time, the most traumatic event of my life. It was like a doctor telling me I had cancer. Worse than that . . . that one of my kids had the disease.

Looking back, though, I think it's probably the best thing that ever happened to me. It woke me up to so many things.

When things go well, we take them for granted. We think that's the way they're supposed to be.

Life isn't made up of any "supposed to bes." There ain't a thing in this world that's "supposed to be." There's not supposed to be a good day. We have the opportunity to make it good. It's not automatic. We have to make it beautiful.

I have no idea how long I can manage. I used to be convinced I could do it till I was seventy. I'm fifty-six now. I'm not good at math, but I know there are a whole lot of "one days" between now and then.

I can't promise that I'll make it and I can't say that I won't. I know I'd like to stick around long enough to pass John McGraw for second on the all-time win list. That's always been the pot at the end of my rainbow. That still hasn't changed.

But there's a long way to go. There are too many "one days" now even to worry about McGraw.

If I can make it through 1990, I think I have a chance. That's the true test. If I find I can't tolerate losing, however, I'll leave the game in a couple of years. I could not continue under false pretenses. I could not take money for merely going through the motions. The Tigers and baseball have been too good to me. I could not cheat the game. I could not cheat the fans.

I think I can whip the demon. I think I can accept the challenge of preparing my teams to perform at their highest levels. I can walk away proudly knowing that, win or lose, I gave it my best. At least I've got a goal.

Coming Back

Throughout my career I've set a lot of goals. I've been lucky to reach almost every one. My first was to make it to managing in the major leagues. After winning a World Series in one league I wanted to be the first to win one in both. It was the same for winning 100 games in a season and 800 games in each league.

I don't mean that to sound egotistical because I believe we all should set goals. Goals give us a sense of direction. As long as they're healthy, they establish self-worth.

To reach this one, though, is the biggest challenge of my life. If there were never another award or prize of any kind, winning this battle would be the biggest victory of my life. Because if I do, I won't be a hypocrite when I tell players that there's no dishonor in losing as long as you give it your best.

I don't want to be a hypocrite. I want to be able to work as hard as I can and then be able to accept the consequences whatever they may be. I know if I can do this I'll make my family feel really proud. I want my kids to look at their dad and my grandkids to look at grandpa—win or lose—and know that he's fine.

That's my biggest challenge. I'm fighting hard to achieve it . . . one day at a time.

Sparky

Billy Schuster used to play shortstop for the Angels about forty-five years ago when Los Angeles had a team in the Pacific Coast League. He had a cup of coffee with three different big league teams. Most of his time was spent in the minors.

Schuster wasn't a great player. But all the fans loved him. People called him "Broadway Billy." They called him that because they never knew what to expect from him. Broadway Billy was an actor on the field. He used to put on quite a show.

When I was a kid growing up in Los Angeles, I went to Angels games just to watch him play. Broadway Billy used to stand there at shortstop chewing a big wad of gum and blow gigantic bubbles while the game was going on. I always watched for one of those babies to break when a line drive went screaming at him. But it never happened. He always had that bubble under control.

Late in a game once, when the sun was going down, I saw him run out to shortstop with one of those miner's hats that have a light on top. Another time after hitting a ground ball to the second baseman, he raced to third base instead of first. The papers the next day reported that he said, "I knew I was out if I ran to first. I figured he'd never throw the ball to third."

Broadway Billy was a little goofy. He loved to give the fans a show. I loved the guy. I loved the way he busted his butt on every single play in every game. He never cheated anyone. Everybody got their money's worth. He was a flat-out hustler.

Broadway Billy died on June 28, 1987, in El Monte, California. He was seventy-four.

After reading that he'd died, I thumbed through a record book to check out his stats. The numbers were amazing. They weren't that good. In fact, they were borderline ugly.

His big league totals sent me scurrying to my page in the record book. The similarities were spooky.

Broadway Billy had a brief but inglorious major league career. Mine was brief and a little more inglorious.

Broadway Billy played a total of 123 major league games in parts of five different seasons. I played one year in the big leagues and appeared in 152 games. Broadway Billy finished with a .234 average. I was slightly close to horrible at .218. He must have blindly run into a fastball once. He had one home run. I kept my eyes open at all times. I never hit one.

Broadway Billy scored 27 runs and knocked in 17. I had him there. I scored a grand total of 42 and doubled his RBI count with a whopping 34.

More haunting than those numbers were the other vital statistics. Broadway Billy was listed at five foot nine and 164 pounds. I'm five-nine and skip around anywhere from 165 to 170.

I never met Broadway Billy but I loved the guy more than he could possibly have ever known.

When I was a kid we played pickup games in the playgrounds. We started right after breakfast and didn't quit till the sun went down. Right after we chose sides the next thing we'd do was pick a player we pretended to be for the day.

I always picked the same guy. I always pretended to be Broadway Billy Schuster.

I guess kids have always pretended to be someone else. It's a harmless fantasy. A way to set goals. A way to grow up.

Grown-ups have dreams, too. Sometimes they even play make-believe. Once in a great while, though, make-believe becomes real.

I'm living proof. I'm Sparky Anderson.

I was born George Lee Anderson. The only nickname I had while I was growing up was "Georgie." To this day, my mom and Rod Dedeaux still call me Georgie. Rod coached baseball at the University of Southern California and became my second father while I was a batboy there.

The name "Sparky" started simply as a joke. Sparky was created in 1955 when I played at Fort Worth in my third year of pro ball. I didn't have a lot of talent so I tried to make up for it with spit and vinegar. I spent more time arguing with umpires than I spent on the bases. My reputation grew fast.

There was an old radio announcer whose name I don't remember. He liked to spike his coffee, but he still kept a pretty quick mind.

"The sparks are flying tonight," he'd say after I charged another umpire.

Then I'd do it the next night. And the next. Finally he got to saying: "And here comes Sparky racing toward the umpire again."

The name stuck. After a while that's all those people called me. I played in Montreal the next year and the name went with me. At first I was embarrassed. Eventually I got used to it.

When I made it to Cincinnati as a big league manager, I went back to signing "George Anderson" on baseballs for the first two years. Finally the public relations department insisted I sign "Sparky."

"Nobody knows who George Anderson is," they said. So I started signing "Sparky."

What started as a harmless joke, though, evolved into a real-life character. Sparky became more than a funny name. He became a real-life cartoon. With his snow-white hair that's made him look sixty for the last fifteen years, his craggy face, and his penchant for turning a simple question into a twenty-minute lecture, Sparky became baseball's unofficial spokesman.

With a media hungry for heroes who can make people laugh, Sparky was turned into a celebrity. For the last twenty years it's been impossible to pick up a baseball magazine without seeing Sparky's face or reading about the world according to Sparky.

Sparky is quoted in newspapers across the country. He does radio and TV spots from New York to Waterloo. He's done national late-night talk shows and has even appeared on a couple of network TV comedy shows.

Sparky can communicate with the common people. So a lot of big companies have spent a lot of big bucks to have Sparky say nice things about their products. Some only want him to shake a few customers' hands.

I'm not lock-cinch sure what it is about Sparky that's made him the character he's turned out to be. You can take him seriously or with a chuckle. But I do know for sure that Sparky loves the stage. He's P. T. Barnum in a funny little cap and knickers.

Managing in five World Series and winning three certainly went a long way to make Sparky the character he is today. Managing a few All-Star Games and winning some Manager of the Year Awards also didn't hurt.

Mama didn't raise no fool. Nothing substitutes for the power of winning.

Society is funny that way. To the victor goes a soapbox. The winner is free to jump aboard and rattle on about anything he chooses without having to know a thing about which he's talking. The soapbox not only goes with the territory, society almost demands it.

Giving a soapbox to Sparky is like giving James Bond his license to kill. Sparky has an opinion on everything from a first-inning hit-and-run to a fourth-quarter jump shot.

Sparky has been a wonderful friend. I love the character very much. He's taken me places I never dreamed I'd reach. He's provided my family with things we never imagined we'd share.

He's a cross between the fact of all those World Series and the fiction of a character that's really make-believe.

What still amazes me after all these years is that the difference between Sparky and George is as great as the difference between fact and fiction.

Sparky lives in the limelight. He doesn't have a choice. George prefers to live quietly at home. At home he has every choice.

Sparky lives surrounded by crowds. George loves being alone with family and friends.

Sparky is expected to be clever and say all those funny things. George is very shy. He loves the freedom of being himself.

Sparky is the myth some people call a legend. George is the real person. He's all I want to be.

The one bond Sparky and George share, however, is their feeling toward people. Both love people. Both insist on being nice. That's the quality about Sparky of which I'm most proud.

The most important lesson my daddy ever taught me was always to be nice to people.

"Being nice to people is the only thing in life that will never cost you a dime," he said. "Treat them nice and they'll treat you the same. And it won't cost a thing."

During the season I've had to play Sparky. Switching from that character back to George once the season is over is one of the toughest jobs I've ever had to tackle.

I can handle playing the character during the season. Getting back to George, though, creates confusion and pain. For a couple of weeks after every season, my body actually aches.

During the season Sparky's world never stops. It doesn't even take a break. From seven-thirty in the morning with a radio talk show about the previous night's game till long after midnight, every minute is filled. Calls from reporters from around the country. Lunches. Appearances. TV cameras always seem to be around.

Sometimes, I swear, people make the games seem incidental. All they really want is to hear Sparky say something funny. All they really want is to see Sparky perform. Everybody wants something a little bit special. Everybody wants a performance just for them.

I understand the role. I also appreciate the roles other people have. They're only trying to do their jobs. But switching from this Olympic pace to the one that's really me took lots of time and lots of practice. It also took its toll.

After each season I used to travel around the country. I did banquets, commercials, promotions, parties. You name it and I was there. I was all over the place like an egg splattered on a wall. One winter I appeared in twenty-one cities in twenty-six days.

I didn't need to travel. I was making enough money from baseball. I didn't even like to travel. I got my fill of that during the season. I traveled because Sparky craved the audience. He had to keep that body running at full speed.

When I absolutely began to hate all that traveling, I tried something else. I turned to painting. I painted everything that didn't move. I painted my house, my garage, my son's house, my mother's house. I couldn't come up with enough things to put paint on. I painted so much that when I had my garage refinished a couple of years ago, they had to sandblast the door to get all the coats off.

I got dangerous with the paintbrush. I got so dangerous that one winter I fell from the ladder and broke my elbow. I showed up at the winter meetings with my arm in a sling. Carol hardly ever goes to a winter meeting. But she went down to San Diego just to help me dress and get around.

When I figured painting had become dangerous to my health, I got involved with something that kept my feet on the ground. I tried gardening. In my case that was picking weeds. That's the only safe thing I know how to do in the garden.

I used to weed my lawn everyday. I actually sat there and handpicked every little weed that dared to show its face. My lawns were absolutely the most weedless property you ever saw in your life.

When I figured we had all of our weed problems solved, I moved inside. I became the official wintertime house cleaner. I washed windows. I scrubbed floors. I vacuumed carpets. I was Mr. Clean.

When there was no more to clean, I went to my son's house and did the same thing. I had it so clean it started to smell like a hospital. He finally asked me to stop showing up all the time.

A few years ago I played golf in the off-season with comedian Flip Wilson. Flip is a talented performer. He's also one of the most respected professionals in show business. I asked him what he felt was the biggest problem in his profession.

Without hesitating a moment he said, "Too many performers don't know when to leave the stage."

"When I'm performing," he said, "I don't let anyone come into my dressing room. Not before I go on the stage and not after. That's because I'm a different person then.

"After I've showered, changed my clothes, and walk out the door, then I'm ready to meet my friends. Now I'm back in the real world. Now I'm the real me. I'm not when I'm on that stage and I know it."

I never forgot that. But I always found making the transition from Sparky to George the toughest thing I've ever had to do.

I think it's because I've never considered myself a celebrity.

I'm just a kid who loved baseball more than anything else in life. Being a celebrity was something I was never prepared to do. I never even wanted it. I've never been able to accept what people think I am. Or more important, what they think I should be. I've got to answer to the whole baseball world.

What people don't understand is that Sparky is as much like George as coal is the color of my hair.

I'm always amazed at the way people treat Sparky. I've never gotten used to some of the things people try to do. At a restaurant, for instance, people think Sparky shouldn't have to pay. Sparky isn't supposed to wait in lines. And people want to give me things as if I were a kid at Christmastime.

I know this goes with the territory. I know people are only trying to be nice. I don't make a fuss, but I've never learned to live comfortably with the special attention.

I've made damn sure, though, never to abuse any of it. Never have I exploited it. Never have I hurt or embarrassed anyone for it. During the off-season, Carol and I eat most of our meals at home. Our big night out is a steak at The Sizzler. If service happens to be slow one night, I never complain to the waitress. Maybe there are problems beyond her control. Maybe the cook decided to take a hike.

It doesn't matter what the reason is. What gives me the right to complain just because I'm Sparky?

I'm the same way in the clubhouse today as I was when I was a rookie player at Santa Barbara in 1953. I clean up my office every day. I'll do it till I retire. If there's a mess then I made it. It's my mess and it's my job to clean it.

I'll never forget the All-Star Game I managed in Kansas City. All of the equipment bags were stored under the team bus. When the game was over and we got back to the hotel, no bellmen were around.

I opened the doors to the luggage compartments and started to remove the bags. Reggie Smith was one of the National League outfielders. He was standing next to me.

"What are you doing, Skip?" he asked when I started to unload the bags from under the bus.

"Well, Reggie, we have one of two choices," I said. "We can get this stuff out or we can stand here all night and look at it."

I love the role of Sparky. I enjoy the character a lot. I appreciate what he's meant to me and my family. Eventually, though, even Sparky met his match. If you call someone stupid long enough, even the brightest person will question his ability to think. If you treat someone special long enough, eventually that person will become convinced he's capable of doing things other people can't.

The mind gets tricked into believing what it hears all the time. Even Sparky got tricked. All the good things that had happened to Sparky and all the special treatment he had received tricked him into thinking he was invincible.

I was already an impassioned winaholic. Coupling this false sense of invincibility with my inability to accept a loss was a lethal mix.

It was a blend of Texas medicine and railroad gin. They strangled up my mind. It got so twisted I actually thought I could will a team to win. It didn't matter how much or how little talent a team had. Sparky could make it work. He would make something happen.

In 1989, I was faced with a losing team. My team played hard. It didn't want to lose. It's just a fact of baseball life. First-place clubs finish first. Last-place clubs finish last.

When my team was struggling, I became paralyzed. People expected me to wave a magic wand. Everything would be all right. Sparky would think of something. Worse than that, I believed it myself. I fell into the same trap. I kept waiting for Sparky to do his magic. Nothing ever came.

That's because there is no magic in Sparky. He's no different than anyone else. If he has a first-place team, he'll make sure that team finishes on top. If he has a last-place team, Sparky can't change that reality.

Nobody thought Sparky could stumble. Nobody thought the pieces could break and completely fall apart. Nobody thought Sparky would ever have to leave his team in the middle of a season to put all the pieces back together again.

But it did happen on May 19, 1989. It was the worst experience of my life and the best thing that ever happened to me.

Facing reality for the first time was painful. It was also a baptism into a fresh new world. For the first time since this whole Sparky thing started, I realized I didn't have to be anything but myself.

Happiness, I learned, can't even begin until you accept yourself. That's what I did in the summer of 1989. That's when I went back to the person I know I really am.

I think Sparky was needed for a long time. I think he served his purpose. Those times of Sparky were marvelous. They were good for me and I hope good for all the fans.

Now I have to let him go. Now I realize that happiness is impossible to achieve if I can't be myself.

For twenty years I've lived with the harness of having to be what people expected of Sparky. For twenty years I tried to live up to an image of a character that isn't anything at all like me. Now I don't want to be anything but me. I'm tired of being something everyone expects me to be.

That doesn't mean I won't be a nice person. When you get right down to it, George is a nicer person than Sparky. George has a genuine, beautiful caring feeling for people. He's more sensitive toward people than anyone realizes.

He just isn't the outgoing personality that Sparky's had to be. George is not the celebrity Sparky is. But who cares about being a celebrity anyway? What's all that stuff going to do anyway? It won't put you in heaven. George can get there just as well as Sparky. In fact, George has a better chance because he takes time to worry about other people instead of worrying about an image.

George is a human being. Nothing more, nothing less. He is not a savior or miracle worker. For too many years I put too much weight on my shoulders trying to be the person everyone wanted me to be.

If I'm lucky enough to go into the Hall of Fame I want to go in as George. Sparky helped to get me there, but George is the one who will make it.

In fact, I think George can become a better manager. I think I've got a chance in the next ten years to be a much better manager than I ever was in my first twenty years. Now I don't worry about all the glitz and glamour that surrounded Sparky. Now all my energy is directed at the team. I don't have to worry about what Sparky is expected to be. I don't have to be what people want me to be. All I have to be is myself. I may not win as many games as before. But I know I'll be a better manager.

I haven't learned any new tricks for becoming a better manager on the field. I've learned a few that help to keep George a little more in control. A winaholic the size of Sparky doesn't just decide to change. I've got to have a plan of attack. I've got to work on it one day at a time.

It's just a simple thing . . . but something as small as room service on the road has been an enormous tool. The way I was raised, room service was for the fancy people. I never felt comfortable ordering something to be brought to my room.

But I wish I would have started a long time ago. Now I order breakfast for my room every day. It gives me the chance to prepare quietly for what I must face that day without the hassle of playing Sparky in the coffee shop before I get my head straight.

I've also changed how I handle requests for interviews. I enjoy my relationship with the media. I think the media enjoys working with me. I understand the reporter's role. I try to help them as much as I can. With the way I like to talk, I don't think that will ever change.

In the past I used to fill every request for every little interview from every little TV or radio station or newspaper from anywhere in the country. Even during a World Series, I would run all over creation trying to fill every request. I was a runaway taxi. I ran downtown, uptown, across town, out of town. I did morning shows, afternoon shows, late shows.

I still fill almost every request. But there's one big difference. Now I do them all at the park. If they can't be done there, then they can't be done. I no longer return every call I receive from every Johnny-come-lately.

My friends know they can count on me for favors. But I no longer feel obligated to everyone who just wants to use Sparky. Those aren't friends. Those are users. They're leeches looking for a little piece of blood.

Carol used to warn me about them all the time. All they wanted was to use me. Even Sparky knew it. He just didn't know how to say no.

I stole time from my family to give to the users. That's time I still feel guilty about. It's also time users will never see again.

Unless it's a request for kids or a worthy charity, my time now belongs to my family. I just say no. The real people understand the situation. The phonies are the ones who have the problem. I should have made it their problem a long time ago.

Going home last year opened my eyes to the people who do care. It's a wonderful feeling to know people respect anything I might have done to help the game.

Maybe it's because I've been in it for so long, but I don't think people really care where I happen to be managing. The uniform itself makes no difference at all. I think they now look at me as part of the game. Winning is no longer the only yardstick. It's how I conducted myself along the way.

Casey Stengel didn't belong any more to the Yankees than he did to the Mets. And he didn't belong any more to either than he did to the game. He just happened to be with those teams. Casey belonged to the game.

I would never equate myself with Casey. I simply appreciate the feelings fans have shared with me. I want to return these good feelings by staying in the game for a long time. But I have to do it with George in control.

Sparky

Once upon a time there was a shortstop named Broadway Billy Schuster. Once upon a time there was a character named Sparky. Both were good and served the game. Now it's time for George.

He's a pretty good guy, too.

Growing Up

There's a joke that the best part of being raised in the ghetto is getting out of it.

I won't say I wish I was back in the ghetto. But I wouldn't trade my childhood with any prince.

I was born in the ghetto. Raised in the ghetto. Learned in the ghetto. I'm proud of where I came from. You couldn't pay me enough money to give up even one day.

I mean no disrespect for parents who are able to provide their kids with luxuries. Now I'm in a position to do those things myself. But learning to live without gives a person so much more appreciation for what he has. I learned quickly that I had to fight for what I wanted. Then I had to fight to keep it. It's a little more of a struggle, yet it makes everything so much more worthwhile.

I've always maintained the best athletes usually come from the ghetto. They know they have to fight to get to the top. They already know nobody's handing them a gift. They don't run scared. That old saying was made for them: When you ain't got nothing, you got nothing to lose.

We didn't have a lot of money, but we were not what you would call poor. I ain't lying when I say we were rich in love. We lived together and we stuck together.

We lived in a two-story house. In the summer it was beautiful. The winters were brutal. We slept upstairs and I swear there were icicles inside the house. All we had was a potbelly stove on the first floor. When it came time for bed, we had to pile on all the blankets we had.

We played hockey on the pond across from the Catholic church. We never had skates, and we used a can for the puck.

There were nine of us—my father, LeeRoy; my mother, Shirley; Grandma and Grandpa Anderson; my oldest sister, Beverly; then me; my brother, Billy; then sisters Carolyn and Sharon.

My mother and father were absolutely the most beautiful people ever to walk on this earth.

I was born in Bridgewater, South Dakota, on February 22, 1934. That's George Washington's birthday, but I'm sure Mama didn't name me George with any illusions I'd grow up to become the president. A major league manager was even further from her mind.

Bridgewater had a whopping 632 people. We had one of the biggest families in town. My grandfather was a housepainter. My daddy painted silos and barns. He also worked part time for the post office.

My daddy was the toughest man I ever saw in my life. He wasn't mean. He was just lead-pipe tough. He got into some of the nastiest fights you could ever imagine. He taught me never to run scared. If you start running scared, you'll be running your whole life.

Daddy was as wise as an owl. He was shy. He kept to himself. He didn't bother anybody. But he didn't want any bother himself. If someone said the word *fight*, they'd hit the ground before the *t* got out.

Daddy didn't want us fighting, but he made the message clear. Don't let anybody push you around. If you have to fight, make that first punch count. If you hit someone hard the first time, you ain't got no fight. It's history.

The same holds true when you meet someone. Daddy said when you shake a man's hand, shake it like you mean it. When you squeeze that hand, let him know you are strong. If you hand a man a dead fish, you're telling him you're weak. Don't look sideways. If you look away, that man questions your strength. If you look him in the eye, you've taken command.

Daddy wasn't talking about physical strength. He was talking about a person's innards ... a man's spirit. That sounds so simple, but it really means so much.

I practice that all the time. When I go to home plate to exchange lineups with the other manager before a game, I shake that man's hand with some life. I want him to know I'm ready to play a game hard. It doesn't matter if we're in first place or down at the bottom. For that day, he's in for a get down and dirty game.

When I meet someone for the first time, I put some meaning into my handshake. I want that person to know I care about him. I represent baseball and the Detroit Tigers. I want that person to be proud of that representation.

It's just a little thing, but life is made up of a million little things, and my daddy taught me to take charge of them.

Daddy was rock hard on the outside. Inside, though, he was a marshmallow. He was such a gentle person. He loved his family. He treated everyone with dignity. He knew the true meaning of love.

I was eleven years old when he taught me the greatest lesson I ever learned.

"Everything in life will cost you something except for one thing," he told me. "And that's to be nice to people. That's the only thing in life that's free. It'll never cost you a dime to be nice. And you'll feel good."

It's true. I retained a lot from my father. But those are the greatest words he ever shared with me. I practice them every single day. When you look at me today, you're looking at my father. We're identical twins, inside and out. I have pictures of him hanging on my wall. People swear they're looking at me.

I can't say that Daddy taught me any of the technical parts of baseball or of managing. But my overall personality and approach to handling people I got from him. That makes me proud. It also gives me a tremendous amount of confidence knowing that Daddy would have done it this way.

My mother is very shy. Very quiet. She won't say "boo" till someone asks. Then you see how wise she really is. I wish everyone had the chance to share her wisdom.

Growing up gave me so many good memories. When times get tough, I find myself drifting back. I can picture that whole city just as if I had been there last week. I can see our house and the Catholic church we went to. I never liked schoolwork, but I liked going to school and being around the other kids. I always remember the jailhouse that was never locked. Nobody even had a key.

I was a skinny little kid with unbelievably big ears. When I was only six years old, my ears were the size they are now. My mother tried to tape them down. I guess she thought if they learned to stay close to my head they wouldn't look so big. But it never worked. They kept popping out. They looked like a pair of saucers.

I look at old pictures now and laugh out loud. I don't remember anybody teasing me about it. My Dumbo ears never bothered me. In fact, nothing did.

We did our share of mischief. But we never tried to hurt anybody. I remember once when some of my friends and I took some weeds that looked like tobacco up to the loft in the old barn we had. We sat there smoking that stuff when all of a sudden the straw caught on fire. We ran out, and before we knew it, the whole barn burned down. Nobody was hurt. At least not from the fire. My butt took a Mike Tyson whipping, though.

There was a family named Pearson in our neighborhood. I have no idea what they did for a living, but all of us kids thought they were rich. The Pearsons were the only family in town that had an indoor bathroom. This was a real bonus when Halloween came around. The big thing for kids on that night was to snatch away as many outhouses as we could and line them up on Main Street.

My grandfather used to sit in ours with a shotgun. We didn't have much, but nobody was going to get our outhouse.

My daddy was a catcher on the semipro baseball team. I remember going to all his games and watching how hard he played. I was just nine when we moved to Los Angeles so I never played in organized leagues in Bridgewater.

In the summer, though, we played pickup games from morning till night. Daddy played catch with me. He must have hit me a million pop flies.

I remember more about South Dakota than any part of my life. I remember all the sights, the sounds, the smells, the people. Maybe I remember Bridgewater so well because I was so happy. It wasn't till managing took its place that I was ever so happy again.

We cut a pretty deep slice into Bridgewater's population when the nine of us moved to Los Angeles.

We moved into a house that had two bedrooms so my parents divided us up as best they could. My brother and I shared a bedroom with my grandparents. My two baby sisters slept in the other one with my parents. My oldest sister slept on a pullout couch.

We had one bathroom, but at least it was indoors. My mother kept her washing machine on the back porch. Eventually we put a bed back there so my brother and I could move out of my grandparents' room.

The house was small. But I never thought anything about it. That's probably because I was rarely there. Until I was thirteen, I never played in any organized sports leagues. From eight o'clock in the morning till suppertime, we played pickup games of baseball, basketball, or football. We played more than any kid in a league.

After dinner we played baseball with a tennis ball across the street in front of Ralph's Market. There was a light in front of the market, and we played till it was bedtime or we broke another light. I can't recall how many lights we broke; I do remember the lickings.

Basketball was my favorite sport. I loved putting up the points. I won't say I was a ball hog. But if I didn't put up forty shots a game, I felt cheated. I figured if I put up forty and half of them went in, I wound up with forty points. Why not? Somebody had to score them. I figured it might as well be me.

I played varsity basketball in my sophomore and junior years. We won two games my first year and jumped all the way to six in my second. I quit in my senior year to concentrate on the baseball team, on which I played varsity for three years.

My high school baseball coach was Bud Brubaker. Bud was also a referee in the National Football League and eventually became head of all the referees.

I have a tremendous amount of respect for Bud because he taught me that when you go out on that field, it's to take care of business. He wasn't mean. But he didn't stand for baloney. You play by the rules and you play hard.

Bud is a gentleman in the true sense of the word. He taught me that to be a professional you must act like a professional.

I never played football in high school because I didn't see any sense in getting hammered by those big linemen. Georgie might have been small, but he was no dummy.

In the summertime I played baseball for Crenshaw Post No. 715. We won a national American Legion championship in 1951. The championship was played at Briggs Stadium, which is now Tiger Stadium. In 1971 when I was with Cincinnati, I returned to Detroit to manage the National League in the All-Star Game at Tiger Stadium. It was almost make-believe.

Looking back, I think my biggest break in baseball came when I was nine years old. We had just moved to Los Angeles and I was walking home from my first day of school. We lived only a few blocks from the University of Southern California. A ball came flying over the fence where the baseball team was practicing. It landed in the bushes. The equipment man gave up looking for it after a while.

I fished the ball out and walked into the practice. I walked up to the first man I saw.

"Who's the boss?" I asked. "This ball came over the fence and I want to give it to the boss."

The boss was Coach Rod Dedeaux. I had no idea I was talking to him.

"You're an honest young man," he said as he took the ball from me. "Do you live around here?"

I told him I lived only a few blocks away, and I wanted to be a batboy. I told him I'd do anything he said.

"You come here every day after school," he said. "But there is one rule. I'm going to check your report card every time it comes out. It better be good or I'll find another batboy."

I had to scuffle for my grades. But I kept them decent enough to remain a batboy for six years. Those were some of the happiest days of my life.

Coach Rod Dedeaux always was and always will be special to me. To this day, he and my mom still call me Georgie. Whenever I get a letter from him, it's addressed to Georgie. He took me under his arm and became my second father. He taught me more than baseball; he helped me become a man.

I always was intense about playing baseball. Coach Dedeaux taught me another dimension. He taught me enthusiasm. There's a difference.

Coach Dedeaux is one of the most enthusiastic persons I've

met in my life. He's close to eighty years old and he's still one of the most positive persons on the face of this earth.

Intensity is fine. He taught me it's also good to smile. He's a genuinely happy person. He calls everybody "Tiger," and he's got a smile for all of them.

Coach Dedeaux's teams have won eleven NCAA baseball championships. That's more than any coach in history. The young men who were fortunate enough to play for him learned a lot more than baseball from him before leaving USC.

Not only was I the batboy, but the football coach let me help out at his team's practices. At the secret practices for the Rose Bowl, I used to return punts and catch extra points.

During the basketball season I caught free throws for Bill Sharman. He used to shoot about a hundred a day. I got to know all the great athletes at USC.

I never spent a day in college. But about ten years ago, the school gave me the Tommy Trojan Award. Throughout my career I've been fortunate to receive my share of awards. This is the one I cherish the most.

Always being around those great athletes put me in a different world. I got used to hanging around older players. It helped me to mature.

The high school in our neighborhood didn't have a baseball team, so I went to high school in a different district. I had my choice of Dorsey or Manual Arts. I chose Dorsey because during the summer, I played ball with some of the kids from there.

Dorsey was in a more affluent neighborhood. I noticed the difference when I first started going to school dances. Until I went to Dorsey, it never dawned on me that we didn't have much money. I was always so busy playing sports, it never occurred to me what other kids did.

A lot of guys at Dorsey drove cars. I went around on busses. I always had to double date with someone who had a car. I chipped in for gas because I never drove. It's hard to drive when you don't have a car.

I realized we were poor the first time I took out Carol. This is the same Carol I've been lucky enough to call my wife for thirty-seven years. Her father drove me home after our date. I had him drop me off a few blocks from home. I pretended to walk into a different house because I didn't want him to see where I lived.

Lefty Phillips is the man I owe my baseball career to. When I was a kid, he was a part-time scout for Cincinnati. He and Coach Dedeaux taught me everything about the game.

I was fourteen years old when I first met Lefty. I think he liked how hard I played the game, so he took me under his wing. He drove me to my games when they were across town. He taught me a lot of little tricks about the game. Lefty and I would sit for hours at the playground just talking about baseball.

Lefty even got me a summer job in Orroville, up in northern California. It was at a box factory, where I spent afternoons loading lumber into boxcars for $1.50 an hour. Four nights a week I played ball in a semipro league.

After high school, Coach Dedeaux wanted me to go to USC. I didn't go for a couple of reasons. I couldn't have gotten in if my uncle had been the dean. More important, I really had no interest in school.

By the time I was in my senior year, Lefty had joined the Dodger organization as a scout.

I had a few clubs interested in signing me. They came to my house and tried to wine and dine my parents and me. I probably could have gotten a few more dollars to sign with another club. But my daddy and Lefty had instilled a sense of loyalty in me. I didn't feel I could sign with anyone but Lefty, who was responsible for making me become the player I was.

So in February 1953, I signed my first professional contract with the Dodgers for $2,400. I didn't think there was that much money in the world. That was $1,200 for a signing bonus and $1,200 for the season. Lefty also promised my dad I'd be sent to Class C ball in nearby Santa Barbara, California.

I have no regrets. Loyalty paid dividends. Things never would have worked out the way they did if it wasn't for Lefty.

I thought of him when I made a move in the 1970 World Series that meant absolutely nothing to the outcome. It was the fifth and final game. Baltimore was putting us away for good, 9–3. Pat Corrales was our back-up catcher. He had worked hard all year.

When you're a back-up to Johnny Bench, you don't see much action, but Pat never complained. He was loyal and so I thought I owed him something. I sent him up to pinch hit so that he could always say he played in a World Series.

When my first pro season ended, I experienced fear for the first time. I had saved most of my signing bonus because I knew I was getting married after the season. Now that season was over, and I didn't have a job. Until then, life had been one big game. All I did was move from one sport to another. Now I was getting married and I was scared.

I saw a Help Wanted sign at Virtue Brothers. They made dinette sets. I didn't even own one, but I got the job of fastening legs onto the tables. I worked on the line opposite a young man from Utah. He put on one set of legs. I put on the other. We worked six days a week with fourteen hours of overtime. I made way more money at Virtue Brothers than I did playing baseball.

When it came time for spring training, I had to make a decision. I remember that kid from Utah asking why I'd leave a job that paid such good money. I wondered myself. But I loved baseball too much to give it up.

The next year I worked in a factory making television antennae for 90 cents an hour. Later I packed boxes for Sears and waxed floors for overtime. I packed doughnuts for Ralph's Bakery, but quit after gaining twenty pounds. Finally I got the chance to play winter ball.

After my first year of managing in the minor leagues, I was a used-car salesman. I was the only salesman who used to talk young people out of buying a car. I knew we had some clunkers and I didn't want to have that on my conscience.

So I've had my share of odd jobs. I know what it's like to scuffle for a buck. I wouldn't trade a minute, though. I'm rich in memories from my entire youth.

I still see a lot of guys from high school when we get together every Thanksgiving morning to play touch football. We gather at eight o'clock at the pancake house down the street from the school. We play the Turkey Bowl from ten to noon. Then we all go home to our families and look forward to seeing each other the next year.

I'm not Sparky Anderson there. I'm still George. No one is treated any differently than the other guy. That's what makes it special. I've been doing this for thirty-seven years. The only ones I've missed were when I was playing winter ball. I look forward to it every year.

I just know my happiest memories come from Bridgewater. I've gone back there about a half a dozen times. I went back three times to help raise money for one thing or another.

They named a baseball field after me—the Sparky Anderson Field. There's a big billboard at the edge of town. It reads, "Hometown of Sparky Anderson." Some people might laugh. But that means a lot to me. That's where my background is. That's where I became George.

My daddy was so proud of that field and the billboard. That meant more to him than all the pictures I've ever appeared in in all of the baseball magazines.

Daddy died on May 17, 1984. The timing was ironic. The Tigers had a Cinderella year. We waltzed through the season. We blew out Kansas City in the playoffs and took just five games to knock off San Diego for the World Championship.

I became the first manager ever to win a World Series in both leagues. Daddy would have been so proud.

Daddy loved baseball so much. He couldn't wait for spring training to come every year. He listened to all the games out on the patio. When baseball came, he was happy for seven months. Without it, I think he became lonesome.

That year would have been so special for him. He always worried more than I did about me getting fired. He never wanted anything bad to happen to me. That would have been a very special season for him.

When Daddy died, I thought a lot about my youth. Once in a while, I still wander back. It's a place that always makes me feel comfortable. It never refuses to let me visit. The welcome mat is always out.

A famous writer once said, "It's a pity youth is wasted on the young."

He wasn't talking about me. I enjoyed every minute.

Managing

I've managed professional baseball since 1964. The last twenty years have been in the major leagues. I've managed in the World Series, League Championship Series, and All-Star Games. I've even won a few Manager of the Year Awards.

I still have trouble explaining exactly what a major league manager is.

He has to know baseball. That's automatic, but not the most important thing. A major league manager has to be a little bit of a lot of things—general, psychologist, confessor, media celebrity, politician, teacher, and most of all friend.

He must know how to get a player to trust him, yet keep that player at least an arm's length away. He doesn't have to be loved.

Yet he must know how to give love. He must not expect to receive respect. He must know how to earn it.

He's managing in the big leagues but he's not a whole lot different from the man in the sandlots. He's a baseball man at heart. He's just got a lot more responsibility to the fans, his employers, his team, and his players.

The manager is the man. He's the one the players and the media come to in good times and in bad. There's a lot of money and glamour that go with the job. There are also a lot more pressures and headaches than anyone could imagine.

It's a good life. But the man better be prepared. If he isn't, he'll be gone a whole lot quicker than the time it took him to get there. And he won't even know what hit him.

Preparation is the single most important duty any manager has. It makes no difference on what level you're managing—major league, minor league, or sandlot. A manager must prepare himself to perform to the best of his ability every single day.

His single most important responsibility is to have his team prepared to play as hard as it can every single day. If the team loses then it's because it simply wasn't good enough. That's all right, as long as it played hard. When it's over, forget it and get ready for the next day.

A manager must recognize the talent his team has and the talent his team lacks. He must take advantage of all the tools his team can offer. Once he makes his decisions, though, he must turn that team loose. And when that game is over, he must prepare them for the next day.

I used to think the great managers could almost will a team to win. I used to think I could do it. I was only fooling myself. Good teams win. Bad teams lose. The manager has the responsibility of preparing his team so that it has a chance to win.

Managing, I believe, is made up of four basic elements: A manager must manage in the dugout, manage his own conduct, understand his players, and deal with the media.

If a manager can't handle all four elements, he has no chance of being great.

THE DUGOUT

Baseball is a simple game. That's what makes it beautiful. That's why it appeals to people of all ages.

Ever since Abner Doubleday came up with the idea, the bases have remained ninety feet apart. The pitcher tries to throw the ball by the batter. The batter tries to hit it over everybody's head. There are four balls. Three strikes. Three outs to each half-inning. Nine innings for each game.

Nothing changes. It's a very simple game. The problem comes up when managers try to show people they're smarter than everyone else.

I've seen it time and time again. Sometimes even veteran managers fall into the trap. It shows up in the simplest situations. Those are generally the type that create the most damage.

Pitching changes are the most common places where some managers try to show they know more than anybody else. The best thing to do is not get tricky. When in doubt, use common sense. It's a friend that rarely betrays you.

I've seen guys bring in a left-handed pitcher to face someone like Don Mattingly or George Brett simply because they bat left-handed. The lefty they bring in might be a turkey who couldn't get his mother out throwing from forty feet away. But they bring him in anyway.

That's foolish. Guys like Mattingly and Brett are going to hit the ball hard even if you kick it up to the plate.

Don't try to outsmart everyone. You only trick yourself. If you've got your top cat out there throwing, let him go. Go home with the lady that brung you to the dance.

Tony La Russa at Oakland is a master. You'll never see him get tricked into lifting Dennis Eckersley from a tight situation. Someone could send up Babe Ruth and La Russa would stick with Eckersley. La Russa doesn't need to show everyone how smart he is by making a move simply for the sake of making it, or by not making an obvious move.

I paid the price for trying to outsmart everyone in the 1975 World Series when Boston sent up Bernie Carbo to pinch hit in the eighth inning of Game Six.

Carbo was a left-handed hitter. I had a right-hander named Rawly Eastwick pitching. I had Will McEnaney warmed and rarin' to go in the bullpen. McEnaney was a lefty.

Eastwick had twenty-two saves that year and McEnaney had fifteen. I had a great one-two punch. But I forgot to throw the punch.

I tried to outsmart everyone by letting Eastwick pitch to Carbo. Carbo hung tough and belted a home run. Boston went on to win. I tried to overmanage and I made everyone pay the price. I forced a Game Seven.

There are no new tricks. Everything's been tried. Good managers are always aware of the situation. For instance, a manager should be able to walk into a ballpark blindfolded in the middle of a game and come close to figuring out the score without looking at the scoreboard.

Give him one inning to check out the defense on both sides. He should be able to come within a couple of runs just by watching the way they set up and how the pitchers are throwing. A good manager doesn't have to be in the dugout to do that. He can do it from the bleachers.

For instance, I start every half-inning by making a quick scan of the defense. I go from right to left. I start at first base and then move around position by position, one by one.

Is everyone where I want them? Should I bring them in or move them back? Does someone need a step to the left or a couple to the right? I paint a picture in my mind. If something is out of place I move it. It's got to look right.

Some of this is instinct. Most of it is training. The good managers discipline themselves so that every possibility is covered. They anticipate every situation in their minds before the play happens. The good ones don't get taken by surprise.

The object of this game never changes. It's the same now as

when Babe Ruth played—score more runs than the other guys and keep them from scoring more than you. How you do that is the trick.

Fans get this part mixed up. Strategy is fine and we should all know how to run a game. But strategy is dictated not by the manager but by the kind of personnel he has. Whitey Herzog is the best man I know at tailoring his strategy to his talent. That's why he is such a good manager.

Whitey never worries about what another team can or can't do. He knows exactly what his team is capable of and he knows how to make the most of it.

It's against every unwritten baseball rule to run when you're three or more runs down. It's suicide. All you do is run yourself out of a scoring threat if your man gets thrown out.

That's part of the baseball book. But Whitey doesn't need any book. Whitey knows his teams. And most of his teams are made up of runners.

If the Cardinals get down by three, they're still running. If Vince Coleman gets on base, you can go to the bank on him stealing second. Now a single cuts the lead to two. If Whitey's pitchers do their job, a late-inning homer can turn it all around.

Whitey doesn't do it just to force something to happen. He knows his teams. He knows when to open it up and when to slow it down. He knows everything that's going on around him at all times.

You don't ask your team to do something it can't. If the manager in Boston, for instance, decides to open up a running game, I have to wonder about him. With that big green wall out in left field, there is only one way to play Boston: swing for the fence.

If you've got a home-run–hitting team, let the boys go out and hack. If they're short on power, try to hit-and-run and mix up the plays. If you've got a hitting team, let the boys swing. If the boys can't hit and you have to rely on pitching, play for a run here and a run there. You might have to bunt more than you normally would.

Once in a while, I'll play a hunch. But all the conditions have to be right. I don't like to make a habit of hunches. I know what my players can and can't do. Rely on hunches long enough and you'll pay for them in the long run. There are a million hunch players in Las Vegas every day. Somehow those casinos manage to stay in business.

Hunches are for losers. Winners prefer preparation. A team may be short in talent, but the good manager has the boys prepared every day to perform to the best of their abilities.

What you have to guard against is trying to do too much when things are going wrong. Everyone has slumps that you can't do anything about. You have to ride them out.

It's the same in all sports. Sometimes the jump shots don't fall. The pucks bang off of the goal posts. The putts don't go in. It happens. You have to recognize a slump and not make matters worse by overmanaging—trying to do too much at the wrong time. A manager can think he can outfox people during these times. What he's really doing is showing off. He is letting his ego get in the way of good sense.

I've been guilty of overmanaging. I did it at Cincinnati but I was lucky. I had a coach there named George Scherger. Every time I got carried away with myself, he'd come into my office and say, "Hey, that isn't going to get it."

We were playing in Houston in 1971. We trailed by a run and put the first two batters on first and second in the top of the ninth. I was going to show the world how smart I was. I put on the hit-and-run so I could catch the whole state of Texas by surprise.

The surprise was on me. The batter hit the ball smack at the third baseman. He stepped on the bag and fired to first for the double play. Now we had a runner on second with two out. The next batter hit an easy fly out to end the game and I walked into the clubhouse with my head hanging.

"You're gonna get too smart for yourself," Scherger said. "All we needed were a couple of flowers, not a whole garden. Remember that the next time."

I appreciated that. I needed it. I learned my lesson. The manager has to let the players play. Don't get things muddy by thinking too much.

Alex Grammas does the same thing for me in Detroit. He corrects me all the time. He's been with me so long, he knows when I'm getting out of line.

Grammas is great for reacting to situations. I may flash a sign for him to give the batter and he might switch it before the pitch is even thrown. Sometimes he'll hear one of the defensive players say something or maybe he'll just sense something on the field. After the inning is over he tells me what happened. A manager is a reflection of his coaches. If he's blessed with good ones, he'd better pay attention.

I learned from Al Lopez that when a game starts look for one thing—pitching. I study the opposing pitcher and mine. I watch every pitch. Nothing is more important.

I make a real study of what the opposing pitcher is throwing. I look for help from my players. I want to hear what they're saying when they come back from the plate. That tells me how I should set up my game plan. Do we play for a run at a time or do we swing away? You can win or lose a lot of games in the first three innings.

All of this I call The Dugout. But it's only 25 percent of the job.

CONDUCT

Conduct in this case does not apply to the players. It applies to how the manager conducts himself as a person.

People might say what difference does that make? All that matters is what happens on the field. Who cares what a guy does away from the park?

That wasn't true before and it isn't true today. In fact, the way a manager conducts himself today is probably more critical than it has ever been. With the tremendous amount of money in today's game, the pressure to perform has become unbelievable. Modern society has created more pressures than players in the past ever had to face.

How a manager conducts his life goes a long way in determining how his players act. If a manager acts like a jerk, chances are his players will act like jerks. If a manager meets his responsibilities and conducts himself with dignity, chances are his players will do the same. Take, for example, the case of Tony La Russa and the Oakland A's.

I'm not suggesting that Oakland doesn't have talented players or that they wouldn't perform without him. But I maintain that his players perfectly reflect his personality and thus he gets the most out of their talent.

Tony is very calm—very intense, very astute, and always aware of the situation. You never catch him running scared. He evaluates the situation and then plans his attack.

It's the same with his team. When you tangle with the Athletics you won't ever get them to run scared. They might lose, but you have to beat them. They don't beat themselves. When it gets down to nitty-gritty time, the Athletics don't panic.

Players are like dogs sensing danger. Some dogs smell it and just go run and hide. Others start to snarl and get ready to attack.

The good manager gives his players every chance to win. That's exactly what Tony La Russa does with the Athletics.

A manager must be disciplined both on and off the field. If he lacks discipline, how in the world can he expect it from his team?

It starts with the little things. Eventually it all gets back to the field. I start with my appearance because that's the image I project. I make sure my appearance is major league before I step out the door. Are my clothes proper? Are my shoes shined? Am I clean shaven? If I'm disciplined personally, I can be disciplined on the field.

That's why I watch the appearance of other managers. I can tell from a manager's appearance at a luncheon, for instance, the kind of discipline I can expect from him on the field. If a guy shows up in blue jeans and a cowboy outfit, I know what to expect from him in the dugout. If he's sloppy in his appearance, I know I've got an edge. Usually that guy must have the best team to win. If he doesn't have the far and away the best, he doesn't have a chance.

That lack of discipline filters directly down to the players. Without discipline, you've got a mess. A manager must sell himself to the players. Obviously, someone with discipline has a lot more to offer.

It reminds me of the story of Fred and John. Both are selling the same product and they start at opposite ends of the block. Fred is selling the product for $10. John is working the other end of the block with a $15 price tag. When the day is over, John has outsold Fred. It didn't matter he was charging $5 more.

That's because Fred sold only the product. John was busy selling himself. That may sound silly, but it's the truth. If you sell yourself first, people believe.

It's the same way in baseball. A manager must sell himself to his players. Then he's got to back up the product he's convinced them to buy.

A writer should be able to go into a clubhouse to interview players and walk away with a great story on the manager without even talking to him. If a writer can't do that, then the manager is a poor leader.

It's the same with successful coaches in all other sports. For instance, if I were writing a story on Lou Holtz, I'd talk to his players. If I wanted to know why Bo Schembechler is so successful, I'd talk to his players. Bo Schembechler could have been an outstanding baseball manager. It just turned out that he happened to select football.

If you look at all the great leaders, you see they're exactly the same. They conduct themselves with dignity. They're always prepared. You'll never catch one of these guys running scared. They're confident in themselves and that confidence fills the players.

UNDERSTANDING

Communication is one of the most overused words in our language. It's also one of the worst words in the book. Communication is what is done on the telephone . . . what you see on TV. It's talking to people. It's listening to what they say.

Understanding is realizing how another person acts and feels. It's appreciating the fact that each human being reacts to situations in different ways. One guy may be motivated by money. Another may be motivated by fear. What turns one person on might turn another off just like a light switch. What causes one player to attack might be the same thing that makes another one want to run.

I don't sit up at night or sit on the bus and dream of things I'm going to say to make my players play better. That's not motivation. Motivation is understanding, and that's why it's the toughest part of managing. Anyone who tells you he's got it completely solved is a liar.

I may not be happy with a certain player and he may not be happy with me. But I won't do anything about it until I walk into my office and talk to the player face to face. I call the player in and give it to him straight. I tell him exactly what's on my mind and I tell him what I want from him. It's the only way I know how to deal with players. You have to be direct with them. You have to be honest.

One of the best responses I ever got out of a player came from Clay Carroll. For a period of five years, he was the best relief pitcher I had.

Carroll was a little different than most guys. He had to

be talked to all the time. He had to be pumped up win or lose.

We called him "The Hawk." He loved it. When I called him into a game, I almost always said the same thing.

"Hawk, you're gonna give me that All-Star performance," I told him. "You didn't make All-Star teams for nothing. You made it because you are the best. That guy at the plate doesn't have any business even being in the same ballpark with you. Now go get him."

And he almost always did. He was amazing. I could see in his face that he loved to be bragged about. It really got him going.

After he saved a game, I would jump out of that dugout and grab his hand really firmly.

"I told you, Hawk," I'd say. "You're the best. This team needs you."

Even after a loss I made sure to talk to him at his locker.

"That wasn't your fault today, Hawk," I'd say. "Those pitches you made were awesome. They just got lucky. But you're gonna get them the next time. They'll pay the price."

If I do anything well at all, I know how to read people. If a guy is a con man, I know he's a con man. Then I treat him like a con man. He may think he's fooling me, but he's only fooling himself. If a guy is straightforward, I treat him in a straightforward manner. You must deal with each person the way they are—not the way you want them to be.

I'm not big on team meetings. I prefer to go one-on-one. I've canceled more meetings in my mind than I've ever had. I've canceled ten for every one I've actually held. I am not a meetings manager.

I've found that when I do have a meeting, I truly had to have that meeting. I don't know about the players, but I had to have it. Something was bothering me and I had to have it out with my guys. But I don't call a meeting until I've had it up to my eyeballs.

In 1973 I called a meeting when we were in Montreal. We were scuffling and playing some very bad baseball.

The night before, Joe Morgan had been spiked and needed several stitches. Johnny Bench had some kind of virus and was throwing up all over the place.

Before the game I called everyone into the clubhouse and shut the door. I don't remember every word I said. And I didn't single out any particular player. But I was screaming.

"If the shoe fits, then wear it," I shouted. "But there's a bunch of you guys who don't want to get into the fight. It's getting tough and some of you are running.

"Now I just want to make this perfectly clear. If you don't want to fight then just let me know. We'll get you out of the way so the big boys can get in and battle. You just let me know because we're not putting up with this stuff no more."

They all got the message. Morgan took the lead and played with the stitches. Bench kept throwing up between innings, but he stuck it out and smacked a homer in the tenth to win the game.

We took off from that point and scrapped hard the rest of the way.

If the players disagree with what I have to say, they can come into my office and talk to me about it the next day. When I'm running a meeting, nobody talks but me. I don't allow an open forum because that never gets anything accomplished.

I walk around the room when I'm talking. I look the players straight in the eye. This sounds impressive, but it only works if you are completely honest with them.

We all have our strengths. We all have our weaknesses. We have moments of bravery and moments of fear. That's because we all are human beings. Problems don't stop just because someone is wearing a big league uniform.

I can tell immediately when a player walks through the clubhouse door with a certain look on his face. I know right away that man has problems at home. I can spot it in a minute. Once I understand that he's got a problem, I can sit and talk with him. I try to get him to understand me. I must make him realize that under no condition will his problem be shared with anyone else. That's automatic.

A manager must understand his players. He must realize that every one of them is human. He must accept their weaknesses along with their strengths. A manager must never allow a player's weaknesses to interfere with the relationship. A manager must be conscious of those weaknesses and ready to trade that player if the opportunity arises. As long as that player is part of the team, though, the manager must not allow those weaknesses to create a disruption.

I am extremely close with all my coaches. But there are things some players have shared with me that I'd never pass along to the coaches. That wouldn't be right. I would never betray a confidence. There are some things I can't share with Tom Monaghan or Jim Campbell or Bill Lajoie.

I never worry if my players are happy. I think any manager who tries to keep his players happy is making a terrible mistake. My responsibility is not to make them happy. My job is to treat them fairly and let them know that when I talk to them, I am telling them the absolute honest truth.

If I set out to make my players happy, we will never win. It is an impossible situation. It can't work because if the only time they're going to be happy is when things are going their way, they're going to be unhappy a lot of the time because things are not going to go their way all the time. I guarantee you that it is impossible to play six months and have everything go right all the time.

It's not my job to make them happy. That's up to them. I'm paid to win and that's what I must concentrate on.

THE MEDIA

This is the part more than any of the others that traps good young managers. It trips up some of the older ones, too. To become a successful major league manager with any sort of longevity, you must be able to deal with the media.

It sounds glamorous. You're on TV all the time. Your picture appears in newspapers and magazines all over the country. You're quoted like some college professor on subjects you might not know a lick about.

It can boggle your mind. I've seen many brilliant baseball men leave the game early simply because they got tired of the hassle.

Sometimes we managers forget that the media has a job to do. Because they're with us every day, it's easy to think that they're part of the team.

They're with the club, all right. But they're not part of the club. They have a responsibility to their newspaper or radio or TV station before they have a responsibility to us.

We must remember that. There are some jerks in the media just as there are some jerks on the ball clubs. But that isn't for us to judge. Whether they're jerks or not, they still have a job to do. And whether we like it or not, our job is to answer their questions.

We don't have to like it. But it's part of the job.

Since I came into the major leagues in 1970, the amount of media exposure has tripled. Sometimes I wonder how some of the old-time great managers would have done if they had had to contend with today's media. Some would have loved it. Casey Stengel would have been even better than he was. Others might have had a problem.

It used to be primarily the regular baseball writers who traveled with the team or the team you were playing. Now we get requests from writers from every part of the newspaper. We get them from the feature section, the business section, the entertainment section, the fashion section. I've even talked to reporters from the food section. That's really funny because the only thing I know how to make is reservations.

They've got another new trick. It's called the "combine." That's where a group of them band together to share all the information they pick up from their teams. In other words, you might say something to the baseball writer in Detroit and he feeds it to the combine. Before you know it, what you said appears in papers all over the country and you might not have wanted it to leave your city.

I remember once in 1985 when we were finishing a home stand. We had the next day off before going on a road trip. Before the game, I told a couple of the writers that Willie Hernandez had a little problem with his arm and I wasn't going to call him in to relieve. I asked them not to write it because I thought with a couple of days rest, Willie might get back in there.

They didn't write it. But the next day when we got to the first stop of our trip—there it was in the out-of-town papers.

The writers kept their end of the deal by not writing what I had told them. But they fed the combine and now the secret was out.

I learned my lesson. Now it's nothing said, nothing written.

Radio talk shows have grown like weeds. They're everywhere. They don't call just from a major league city. They operate out of every city in the United States. Yet, television is what really revolutionized our game. There are morning shows, afternoon shows, late-night shows, talk shows, taped shows, and live shows.

Minicams have reshaped the industry. We take one step over the foul line after a game and, I swear, a camera is staring us in the face. Why did we do this? Why didn't we do that? Sometimes we don't even get a chance to collect our thoughts before we have to replay the whole game.

TV also has affected newspaper coverage. Because TV gives scores and interviews as soon as a game is over, writers are forced to look for a different angle. It isn't good enough now just to report on the game. Now the writer wants to know everything from what you eat for breakfast to the color of socks you wear to dinner.

Digging for stories can lead to trouble. Especially if the wrong guy has the shovel. I remember when I first went to Cincinnati and I was convinced I could conquer the world. I was talking to a reporter from Dayton named Si Burick. He turned out to be one of my dearest friends.

"There are three catchers in this league I know I can steal blind," I told Si in my enthusiasm to be in the big leagues.

"I'm going to run them silly and you can print that."

Then I proceeded to name the three catchers.

"Young man, let me give you a piece of advice," Si told me as he put down his pen and notebook.

"It's the same thing I told the manager before you and the manager before him. Don't say anything to a reporter unless you really want to see it in the paper. Don't say anything about another manager or player. Do it on the field."

I learned a very important lesson from Si. And that was way back in 1970. Now some questions have become downright silly. But they're part of the game . . . part of what every manager faces.

Don't get me wrong. I love the media. I love to talk. I truly enjoy sparring with the press. I honestly think it helps to keep my mind sharp. I enjoy helping the writers, particularly the young ones. I watch them when they walk into my room. I can tell they're shaking in their boots. It's hard for them to believe they're talking to a major league manager. They're so scared sometimes they forget to ask questions.

I always try to give them something. I try to lead them into a story. That's when I run into trouble and start talking too much. Over the years I've had more big stories break in little papers simply because I tried to help a youngster out.

I also know the difference between an A.M. and P.M. writer. The A.M. guy is looking for the straight stuff. That's a snap. The P.M. guy needs a little more feature stuff. Sometimes I have to strain, but I usually come up with something.

I know how tough it can be on some managers. Some guys simply don't enjoy talking that much. Others don't like the feeling of being second-guessed by the media for every little move they make.

Some guys are actually killed by the media. Gene Mauch used to say that he got tired of playing 486 games a year. There were the 162 on the schedule. There were the 162 he played in his mind to prepare for each game. Then there were the 162 he had to play for the media after each game.

I know the media has a job to do. They have to ask questions like they're shooting a machine gun. Maybe all the bullets won't hit. But once in a while, one zaps the target.

My problem is that I talk too much. A writer asks me what time it is and I wind up telling him how the clock is made. I can't count the times my bosses have told me to watch what I say. I used to return every phone call from every writer or broadcaster from any part of the country. I've finally had to stop that now and restrict my media involvement to the times I am at the park.

Fortunately when I talk to the media I can generally control the situation. I know what the reporter is looking for. I know how much I can say. While a reporter is asking me a question, I'm already thinking of an answer. Sometimes I have no alternative. But I hate to say "I don't know" or "We'll just have to wait and see." When I'm asked a question I feel obligated to give an answer. I always run my answers through my mind to picture how they will look in print the next morning.

One thing I never will do is talk a player down. I might say nothing about certain players, but I'll never talk anyone down. When I'm asked something about a certain player, generally I can come up with some lines to make him look good.

That's a trick young managers must learn. If a player is struggling, the manager must know how to keep the media from crucifying him. The manager must make sure the media doesn't destroy a player. Some players can't handle media pressure. Some lose a career from it.

The manager can't lie. But he must be able to manipulate. He's got to take the heat when the player can't. He's got to know how to put out a fire in one spot by starting a new one somewhere else.

I'm usually pretty good with the lines. Don't forget, I sold used cars one off-season.

The Dugout, Conduct, Understanding, and The Media—the big four. If a manager doesn't have all four, he'll never be great. If he's got three of the four, he can be pretty good. Guys with three of the four can last for twenty-five years. Guys with just two don't stand a chance. They'll be around for a couple of years. Maybe five, but that's their limit.

If a guy has just one, he'll be history before the year is over. It won't take long until everyone catches on to his act. The manager is too important to stand there exposed.

I believe that Understanding and The Media are the two most important factors. The Dugout part takes care of itself if you have the right personnel. Conduct is something you have or you don't. There's that old saying that a pig in a tuxedo is still a pig.

Having all four qualities doesn't guarantee a championship. But it certainly puts you a couple of steps ahead of the other guys.

Give somebody like Gene Mauch the best club and it will always win. Same thing with Whitey Herzog. Always, always win. That's because they're so disciplined. They've got great knowledge and great instincts. When they didn't win, that meant they didn't have the best club. It's that simple.

Walter Alston never lost when he had the best club. Casey Stengel never did either. When the great ones had the best clubs, they never blew it.

The guys I mentioned didn't always need the best talent. When they ran into problems, they knew how to pull off a couple of tricks to buy some time till things got straightened out.

I've heard people say that great managers win anywhere from eight to twelve games a year for their teams.

False!

Managing

I don't care who it is. Gene Mauch, Walter Alston, Whitey Herzog, or John McGraw. Even the legendary Casey Stengel never won a game for the Yankees.

Teams get the victories. The only thing a good manager can do is save what his team already has won. A good manager does not hurt his team. He makes sure his team wins the games that are won. He does not make mistakes that lose games that already are his.

I've seen so many guys lose games that their boys had already put into the hopper because they didn't know how to close it. It was wrapped up with a bow on top and they didn't know how to put it away.

All good managers are good defensive managers for the last six outs of the game. The last six outs are the whole game. Everything hinges on them. You might blow out a team once in a while. A few times you're going to get blown out, too. Basically, though, most games are decided in the eighth and ninth innings.

The guy who has a career of not giving them away is going to have a great career. He can last a long time if he knows how to seal them up. The other ones don't last too long. They're fly-by-nighters. Since I started managing twenty years ago, I can't even remember all the guys who have come and gone. They're sort of like pollen when the wind whips up. And a lot of them were blown away because they didn't know how to turn the key.

I love seeing fresh young managers come into the league. I love to see them develop. I think young managers today are much more understanding of players than some of the older guys. In the old days, the manager was the king. He had all the power; a player had no protection at all. A player actually feared the manager. In fact, a lot of times, the manager never even talked to the players. He didn't have to.

When I played, I never talked to the manager. I never even dreamed about it. I never went up to ask him something, let alone express an opinion. The only time he talked to me was to tell me to do something.

That's the difference today. Today the manager had better understand his players. Some of those players are making $3 million a year. If he doesn't understand them, they'll run him out so fast his head will swim. Those players are tough to replace. The manager isn't.

When I started managing, I was only thirty years old. Most of the players I had were older than me. I'd talk to them. And I'd listen. But I was a hotheaded little son of a gun who ran around like a raving maniac. I was just a kid who believed strongly in all my convictions. I believed everything I did was right. It was the only way. I couldn't believe people could doubt my moves.

I did have one gift, though. And that was the greatest gift God ever gave me. I had the insight to understand. I also made the effort to know my players. I always knew that people are crying to be understood. I'm not sure why; maybe it's because I never felt understood.

All I can think is that God must have blessed my mother when I was born and said, "We're going to make him a major league manager. And he's going to manage for a long, long time."

I was only thirty-five years old when I was hired by the Cincinnati Reds. Then I was blessed with players like Pete Rose and Johnny Bench and Joe Morgan and Tony Perez.

The greatest compliment I ever received came from those guys.

"He treated us like men," they said, "not like little boys."

I enjoy talking to young managers. But I give them advice only if they ask. If they do, I tell them—never look upstairs. In other words, don't go running to the front office with your problems. They've got problems of their own. Don't go blaming the front office for your problems. Try to work them out with your players.

If you go running upstairs with every little problem, you're worried about your job. Show the front office you're worried enough and they'll give you something to worry about.

I've never in my life been worried about being fired. If I'm fired, I'm fired. I'll get another job. I'll turn it around to make it their loss. Just because a person is fired, he isn't a bad person. It's only bad if he runs scared. Then he can't do the job he's capable of doing.

The worst mistake a young manager can make is to not be himself. Suddenly he's in the big leagues and he thinks he's got to be somebody else. William Shakespeare had the right idea: "To thine own self be true."

I suppose you can apply that to every walk of life. I know you can apply it to managing in the big leagues. It's the first thing I tell every young manager who asks me the secret for sticking around for a long time. If you're a wild man, go ahead and be wild. If you're a screamer, use those lungs. If you're quiet and more laid back, then do your business that way.

Do it the way you really are. It won't work any other way. If a man has the tools and isn't afraid to be himself, he will succeed.

For instance, I feel much more content now than I ever did in my career. I certainly don't enjoy finishing anywhere near the bottom in the standings. First place or last place, though, I'm going to be myself. My job is to prepare my team—and myself—to perform on the highest level it can, every single day. That level might not be worthy of first place, but it must be the highest we can achieve at the moment.

Once a manager becomes content with himself, he'll perform with more confidence. It's just like a player his first few years up in the majors. At first he cruises along purely on physical talent. Perhaps deep down, he's not sure why he is here. Once he realizes that this is real and he truly does belong . . . look out. Now he's ready to play to his true potential. I try to explain this to all young players and managers.

A good manager must also learn to take a good old-fashioned butt kicking and come out of it with the same pride he had going into the fight. I mean the kind that hurts so bad it's tough to sit down for a couple of weeks. If he can't do that, he's in trouble. If you get whipped, wave the white flag and shake the other man's hand. That man deserves it and there's nothing to be ashamed of.

Every time I've lost a World Series or a League Championship Series, I've walked across that field to shake the other man's hand. He's the king. He whipped me.

It's part of the game. Once a manager learns he has to take his share, he's going to be a better performer. And a better person.

Don't think the best manager always ends up first. I saw Gene Mauch finish fourth and fifth plenty of times when I know he did the best job of managing. He just happened to have a fourth- or fifth-place club. That was the talent level of the players he had. Chances are, he probably got more out of them than what they really had.

That's why Manager of the Year Awards are a joke in a way. They don't tell the real story. A manager knows when he's done the best he can. If he has, there's nothing more he can do.

Managers

Even when I was a player, I had tremendous respect for the manager. Maybe it's because I didn't have much talent, so I got more chances to study him.

Managers are a lot like players. A few are so-so. Most are all right. Some are good. Only a handful deserve to be called great.

The great ones know who they are. They don't have to talk about themselves. Since I faced my problem of accepting losses and started a program to deal with it, my regard for the great ones has grown.

Managing can be painful. Take it from me . . . I know.

All the good managers know the game inside and out. The

great ones take it one step beyond. Yet all the great ones know a manager doesn't win games. Players win. Players lose.

The great ones know how to get the most out of their players. It's like squeezing an orange. The good managers can squeeze out half a glass of juice. The great ones get that glass full. They get their players to do their best every time they take the field.

The great ones don't lose late in a game what their players have already won. If it's won, they don't give it away. Sounds simple, but so many managers get caught giving away what their players already had won.

All great managers are great leaders. Not only do they know baseball, they know men. They would be leaders in any field.

Finally, the great ones are around for a long time. Some guys can turn it on for five or even ten years. The great ones stick around for at least twenty. Nothing substitutes for longevity. Time is the greatest yardstick of all.

Who's the greatest? The record book says Connie Mack. Mack finished with 3,776 victories! He won more games on a professional level in any sport than anybody in history. Forget about catching him. No one will ever come close.

I'll never take any credit away from Mr. Mack. He had to be special to win that many games. Just to stick around for fifty-three years is unbelievable. But his record should stand separate from the rest. Mack owned the club. I don't think he ever worried about getting fired from his job. Mack's team won its last pennant in 1931 when he was sixty-nine years old. He stayed on as manager through the 1950 season, when he was eighty-eight.

I wasn't around when he managed. But I question how much he really managed the last fifteen to twenty years. From some of the things I've heard, I think you have to disregard a lot of those victories. A lot of his coaches actually did the work a manager normally does. At the end of his career, I don't think he was totally running the ball club.

The number one man for numbers has to be John McGraw. This man should be an idol to every manager who puts on a big league uniform. In thirty-three years, John McGraw won 2,840 major league games. Now just imagine. Suppose you owned a ball club and hired a young man who had never managed before. Suppose you told him that you were going to let him manage for twenty-eight straight years. And suppose he won 100 games a season for twenty-eight straight years.

He still wouldn't catch McGraw!

Pete Rose finished with 4,256 hits. That's an incredible feat. McGraw's 2,840 wins are every bit as tremendous as Pete's 4,256 hits.

McGraw has to be placed on a pedestal. Every manager that ever puts on a uniform should try to catch him. They'll never reach him. Just like no one will ever reach 4,256 hits. But 2,840 is the bull's-eye we all must shoot at. I have to admit that passing McGraw remains my dream.

I've been very lucky. I've managed against some of the brightest minds in the history of the game. Some of these guys would have starred in any period of baseball—at the turn of the century, during the dead ball era, the war years, or the present.

Gene Mauch, Walter Alston, and Whitey Herzog were the best. It was an honor to go up against them.

A lot of people criticize Mauch for never winning the prize. He never won a World Series. He finished his career with a losing record. But most of the time he had to manage teams that had their hands full just finishing the season.

Gene Mauch managed almost 4000 major league games. He stuck around for almost twenty-six years. Look in the books . . . there ain't many like that.

A lot of people misread Mauch. They thought he was aloof. They thought he was arrogant. They never knew what really drove the man.

He was one of the most down-to-earth people you could ever meet. Mauch wasn't aloof; he was just so intense. He knew the game better than anyone ever knew the game. In his mind, he could actually dissect every little part of the game and show you how it was all put together.

Because he knew the game so well, he had trouble understanding why it couldn't be played to perfection. He took losses so hard he finally had to get out of the game. The losses crippled his nerves. I know firsthand what that can do.

Mauch was a tremendous innovator. One of the greatest in history. He invented the double and triple switch. Until he did it, it wasn't done.

The double switch is beautiful because it gives the manager so much more flexibility. Say, for instance, it was late in the game and Mauch wanted to bring in a new pitcher. For defensive purposes, he might also want someone stronger at another position.

If the number five man in the lineup made the last out, he put the pitcher in the fifth spot and the other new guy in the pitcher's number nine spot so that the new pitcher wouldn't bat until eight guys took their turn.

The triple switch involved a new pitcher and two new players. The pitcher went into the spot that made the last out and the other two guys would go into the lineup where they would bat first. Now it's done all the time and relief pitchers can work longer.

Mauch took it one step further. If he had a pitcher he wanted to stay in the game except for facing a certain batter, he moved that pitcher into right field for one man and then brought him back in to pitch the rest of the way. He was always thinking, always one step ahead.

Mauch was the finest strategist. He managed baseball like he was going around a Monopoly board. He knew what the other manager had and he knew what he had. He knew if you had the better team or if he had the better team. If you had the better team, then he had to come up with something to make up the difference. If you had the best club, you had a chance to beat him. If he had the best club, you had no chance. If the clubs were even, Mauch had the advantage.

I managed against him for a long time. I always had the better teams. If he would have had the teams I was blessed with, you would have still been counting up the numbers.

I loved managing against Mauch because I had to stay so sharp. If I blinked—bam—it was gone. My wife didn't have to look at the schedule. She always knew when Mauch was coming to town. She could tell because I was happy. She knew I was looking forward to it.

If you studied Gene Mauch closely, he'd teach you how to manage. He made you learn. Because if you didn't, he lost you like a pea in the sand. Boom—it was gone. Now go try to find it. He could lose you so fast, you didn't even know it was gone. He was like a professional pickpocket. He was so good, you wanted to thank him when he was finished.

Mauch taught me one of the greatest lessons I ever learned and it had nothing to do with baseball strategy. My first game as a big league manager was Opening Day 1970 at old Crosley Field. We played the Montreal Expos and Mauch was already known as one of the best managers around. We were standing at home plate for the pregame ceremonies. He looked at me and said, "Enjoy this moment because you'll never pass this way again."

At the time, I didn't know exactly what he meant. I finally figured it out. He was telling me, "I wish you the very best of luck. Just be who you are. Just be George Anderson."

I never forgot that. I never will. I told him that for just one year, I'd love to be on the same team with him. He could manage and I'd be a coach. Or I could manage and he'd be a coach. It wouldn't matter. It would be the greatest learning experience I could ever have.

Even with a lifetime losing percentage, Gene Mauch must go into the Hall of Fame. Until the day I die, I'll use every ounce of influence I have to see that he makes it. If he doesn't make it, then there isn't a manager alive to come down the road who ever should.

Walter Alston is another master I was privileged to manage against. Walter finished with 2,040 wins. He finished with a career winning percentage that was high enough to win a pennant in most years. Alston and Mauch were a lot alike. The only difference was that Walter had those great Dodger teams and Gene had to scuffle almost his entire career.

On the outside, Alston and Mauch were night and day. They would have made the oddest pair of bookends you could imagine. But I know that if you stripped away everything, inside they were exactly the same.

Mauch was the general. Cool. Quiet. Eyes that looked right through you. He saw everything that went on—on the field and in that clubhouse. You couldn't fool him. Once he put on that uniform, he never talked to you. When we played his teams, before the game I waved to him and threw him a salute. He threw one back and that was it. No words. No conversation. It was time to go to war.

At the winter meetings, Gene would sit around and talk all day. As long as it was baseball and you knew what you were talking about, he wouldn't stop.

On the outside Alston was different. He wasn't the general. He was the wise old grandfather. But you couldn't trick him. He also knew everything that was going on.

Alston was the ultimate gentleman. He was tall. Graceful. As soon as he stepped onto the field he had so much presence. In that clean blue-and-white uniform, he was the Dodgers. Before a game, he'd chat a little. But he never tipped his hand. He was cooler than a professional poker player. I always wondered how he could stay so peaceful.

Against those two guys, I knew that if my team was better than theirs and I made all the right moves, I'd win. If their teams were better and they made the right moves, they'd win. I knew I couldn't wait for a mistake from them. I knew I wouldn't get one.

Alston was an excellent strategist. He played chess on the field, but was never fancy. Basically he stayed by the book all the time. He hit you with a bunt when the bunt was called for. If you shut the play down, fine. If you didn't, you lost the game.

He rarely gambled. He'd sit back and force you to make the plays. I knew why.

Walter knew he had great pitching. He believed his pitching could stop anybody so he played for one run at a time. He was very conservative. Some people thought he was boring, but it was because of the staff he had. If he didn't have that staff, he would have managed differently. He painted pictures with his pitchers.

People in the American League office don't like to hear me say it, but baseball is a better game without the designated hitter. The pitcher is the focus of the game and he's never totally in it in the American League. All he does is throw the ball while we send up some gorilla to hit for him.

During the 1974 season, I faced Walter's Dodgers in Cincinnati. Mike Marshall was having a fantastic season and Alston brought him in to shut us down in the ninth.

In the top of the tenth, the Dodgers put runners on first and second with two out. Bill Russell was up. He was their eighth hitter. With first base filled, I ordered him intentionally walked.

Johnny Bench didn't believe it. He wanted to pitch to Russell. With Marshall scheduled to bat next, I figured I'd force Alston to lift him for a pinch hitter.

There was one problem. Walter knew exactly what I was thinking. So he let Marshall bat for himself. We got him out. But it didn't matter.

Walter knew that even if he didn't score then, Marshall would outpitch my bullpen for two more innings and he could steal a run. They did and we lost in twelve.

Walter knew my personnel and didn't panic. It doesn't always work. But it's funny how the great ones seem to make it work most of the time.

Another time he beat me in the first inning in Los Angeles. We put runners on second and third with nobody out. Tony Perez was up. Johnny Bench was standing out there in the on-deck circle just drooling to get at that pitcher.

Walter held up four fingers and sent Perez to first. He knew that for the last ten games, Perez had been destroying the ball like Paul Bunyan chopped down trees. It took some kind of guts to load the bases for Johnny Bench. But Walter knew that if he didn't stop it right then, the game was out of control.

The pitcher got Bench to ground into a double play on the first pitch. They got out of the inning on just one run and we wound up losing the game.

That showed me Alston had no fear. It was just one game. But to this day, that remains a great moment for me.

Walter knew when to open and close all the valves. All great managers do. The great ones know their club. They manage according to the players they have. They have enough confidence in themselves to make adjustments. The other guys try to get their clubs to play according to the way they like to manage. Most of the time, the players can't handle it. It just doesn't work.

Walter understood that. He knew exactly what he had and how to make the most of it. He had a great mind and a keen eye. When he looked out at that field, he knew where everything was supposed to be. He knew how to put everything into place.

Away from the field, Walter had a great sense of humor. He had great insight and really understood human nature.

I'll never forget my first winter meeting as a manager. It was at the Diplomat Hotel in Fort Lauderdale. There's a traditional Tuesday luncheon for the managers with all the writers and sportscasters from around the country. We'd been there a couple of days and Walter kept teasing me that all rookie managers had to get up and give a speech at the luncheon. Back then, I was more afraid of that than facing Willie McCovey with the bases loaded.

Finally, Walter told me it was a joke. Then he made up for it by giving me one of the best lessons I ever learned in life.

When I showed up at the luncheon, the room was packed with

all the managers and some of the biggest sports writers in the country. I knew I didn't have to give a speech, but my knees were still knocking. When I walked in, I saw four managers in the middle of the room carrying on like it was New Year's Eve. They were loud. They had drinks in their hands. They were acting like the high school football hero at the homecoming dance.

I looked around the room for anybody I knew. I spotted Lefty Phillips sitting with Alston in the corner. They waved me over and sat me down between them.

"You sit down here and just take a look around the room," Walter told me. "Just be one of us. You don't have to be out there in the middle. That's not for you. You don't need it. That's not the way."

Walter gave me one of the most important lessons I ever learned. He taught me to be myself. He told me to be proud of myself. He told me to be confident in all my decisions.

"You don't have to be out in the middle of traffic telling everybody how important you are," he told me. "Leave that stuff for the pretenders. They won't be around long anyway."

Walter never had to tell people who he was. He knew all the great things he had accomplished. He was proud of them. But he didn't go around telling everybody. He didn't need to.

I went to a retirement luncheon for Walter in Los Angeles. I sat at a table between Danny Ozark and one of Walter's friends. I don't remember the other man's name, but I'll never forget what he said.

When Walter walked into the room through the back door, everybody stood up and cheered. Walter's friend said; "You know . . . that man came and now he's gone. But he never changed. He's the same now as when he started."

I thought about that for a while and finally realized that was the highest compliment anyone could have paid him. Here was a man from Venice, Ohio. He wound up in Los Angeles and finished with 2,040 wins in the big leagues. And the man never changed!

That's a tremendous tribute. Walter was a tremendous human being.

The best defensive manager I ever went up against was Alvin Dark. I never saw anyone able to protect a lead late in the game like Dark did. Dark always knew who his money pitcher was. This was the guy who wanted to be on the mound when the chips were on the line. You never even knew that guy was in the park until it got late in the game and Dark's team was on top. When Dark was at Oakland, he didn't care where Rollie Fingers was until about the eighth inning.

I could tell when Dark would have him start to loosen up. If he had the lead he refused to let it slip away. He was going to the horse. Wins are too tough to come by and Dark refused to let one slip away.

I attack a game in two stages—the first seven innings and then the last six outs. When it gets down to the last two innings, I count outs. It doesn't matter if we're up or down. I know what I can do with six, five, four, three, two, or one out to go.

Dark was the best when it came down to the final six. He knew how to hold on to the lead when he got to six-out time. You had to get him early. If he had the lead late, you might as well try to beat the traffic. He wasn't about to give it up.

He was amazing. He was a million-dollar watchdog protecting that lead. He was tough to manage against.

Billy Martin was also tough to go up against. Even with all those crazy things going on around him, taking on Billy Martin was always a battle.

Billy was tough because he had no fear. He never ran scared. He had no fear of what he said to the writers. He had no fear of what you said to the writers. He wasn't scared of what his bosses said. And apparently he wasn't scared to tell his bosses what he thought.

When a man has no fear, he's tough to play against. How in the hell can you bluff him into a move he shouldn't make? You can't.

So you better stay on your toes. Your one shot might be your only shot.

On the field he was deadly. He dared you to try something. He dared you to challenge him. The man managed with the best of them.

I love managing against the guy who's worried about his job. I can pick him out in a second. The scare drips from him. He's worried.

"What will the writers write if I make this move?" he asks himself. "What will the fans say tomorrow after they read what the writers write?" He's afraid of his shadow.

This guy is scared and I know I've got him. When it gets down to make-it-or-break-it time, this guy is going to crack. All I've got to do is get him in that position.

You don't see that fear in the great managers. You don't see them running like scared little mice. The great ones are leaders. They're generals. They don't show fear. They're all Pattons. When you're managing, there's nothing worse than looking across the field and seeing Patton in a tank sitting in the other dugout. Now you've got a problem.

I admire Tommy Lasorda. To me, he's the closest thing we have to the Old Man—Casey Stengel. Tommy has such a sensitive feeling for people. It might look like it's all for show. But he's for real. That feeling is genuine. He really does love people.

I don't care what anyone tells me, a manager must love his players and show them that he cares. If he doesn't he'll lose them faster than a drunk loses money. You must have feeling for every player on your team. From the guy who bats cleanup to the bullpen catcher.

Tommy's got that feeling. He's not afraid to show it. He loves all his boys.

He also has great showmanship. Tommy's on stage all the time. Twenty-four hours a day. The game is part of the show and Tommy knows how to play it. He loves being with the beautiful people. He loves hamming it up.

There's nothing wrong with that. It's good for the Dodgers. It's good for the writers. It's good for the fans. It's good for Tommy. And believe me, he knows it.

Whitey Herzog has a little bit of the Old Man in him. He knew the Old Man, he played for him a little while, and he even does a great imitation of the Old Man.

The first game I managed against Whitey Herzog was in the American League at Kansas City. I met him before that but never had managed against him.

Right from the start I could tell he was flat-out good. I could tell that Whitey knew everything that went on out there on the field. The first thing I noticed was the way he used his bullpen. Every time I thought I had him in a position where I could sneak in a certain hitter against him, Whitey was ready with a pitcher to counter the move.

But he never made the move that quickly to waste his pitchers in the bullpen. Sometimes managers waste pitchers having them warm up too much. Not Whitey. He always has them ready just at the time they're needed. Right now, he probably knows the game better than anyone in it.

His record speaks for itself. He won at Kansas City. He left there and turned St. Louis around as soon as he got there. His bags weren't even unpacked. So nothing he does surprises me.

If you give Whitey Herzog 90 percent and the other guy 100 percent, Whitey will win all the time. Give him 80 percent and the other guy wins. But give him 90 and he's a lock. He's that good. He's a cinch for the Hall of Fame.

I enjoy talking to Whitey so much because he knows the game so well. He knows all the players. He knows all their strengths and all their weaknesses. He knows every player in both leagues.

That's why Whitey is such a key to all the Cardinal trades. He and I have a long-standing joke going. Whenever we run into each other or talk on the phone the first thing he says is, "You name the time—East Coast or West Coast—and let's make a deal. Tell me who you want and we'll work it out."

The man knows the game.

There are four young managers today who should make it big before they leave the game—Tony La Russa at Oakland, Jim Leyland at Pittsburgh, Tom Trebelhorn at Milwaukee, and Tom Kelly at Minnesota. In my twenty years of managing in the big leagues, I don't think we've ever had four young managers as bright as these guys.

Now the trick is to stick around and put some numbers on the board. La Russa just crossed that magic line—ten years. That's tough. Now he has to make it to twenty-five. It gets even tougher. It's up to him. He has to be hungry.

I truly enjoy managing against the great ones. I can't imagine a bigger thrill in sports. They know they're good. They know if the guy they're up against is good. I can sense it during batting practice. I'm going over his ball club in my mind. He's going over mine.

Who does he have in the starting lineup? Who does he have sitting on the bench? How am I going to attack his pitcher? How is he going to try to get mine? If he's got Superman sitting on his bench, I can't let Superman beat me. I've got to figure out a way to keep Superman out of the game. If that game is on the line, it's my job not to let Superman beat me. Some other guy might do it. But not Superman. If he beats me, I didn't do my job.

When I manage against these guys, nobody's seeing my number one cat till there ain't nothing they can do to stop him.

The good ones are out to slicker you. They ain't about to be slickered.

There's nothing in the world I enjoy more than going up against one of the Pattons. It's a lot more fun when my army is a little stronger than theirs. But even without that, it's the one thrill that makes me want to come back every spring. It's the closest thing I'll ever get to being in the ring with the champion of the world.

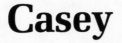

Casey

John McGraw is the man on top when it comes to numbers. He's the prize you shoot for. Gene Mauch and Walter Alston were the best I personally had the privilege to manage against. They knew the game and how to get the most out of what they had better than anybody I ever saw.

Then there's Casey Stengel—"The Old Professor."

Casey finished 914 wins behind McGraw. I never managed against Casey so I can't say for sure about his managing techniques.

I do know one thing. Casey is The Man!

It really isn't fair to talk about Casey together with any other managers no matter how great they were. Casey stands alone. There's Casey and the rest of baseball.

A lot of people might figure I'm wackier than they thought, but to me, Casey Stengel is the most dominant figure ever to bless baseball. To me, Casey Stengel is more dominant than Babe Ruth! We still feel Casey's impact. We always will.

The Babe was something special. He revolutionalized the game with all those monster home runs. He made Yankee Stadium. He played in the roaring twenties when everything was bigger than life. He was as big off the field as he was on it. Books were written about him. Movies were made of his life. Babe Ruth is the one man all players are measured against. He wasn't the best player ever to come along. But no player dominated the game like The Babe.

In my opinion Casey Stengel surpassed all that.

Casey not only was a master at managing, he transcended baseball. His style and personality actually went beyond the game.

Casey put some down-home humor into the game. He was a pioneer when it came to linking baseball and the media. He took the game beyond the box score and the stats.

Nobody was sharper than The Old Man. He was scientist and artist combined. Baseball only happened to be his vehicle. Casey was the master entertainer. He also was a guru on life.

You have to remember that Casey managed some pretty bad clubs at the beginning and end of his career. With decent clubs all the way, he would have sailed way past 2,000 wins. He would have finished right next to McGraw.

Numbers mean nothing when it comes to The Old Man. Throw all the numbers away when you talk about Casey. There never was another manager in history that contributed more to the betterment of the game than Casey Stengel. There never will be.

People use the expression "a man for all seasons." Casey was "a man for all people." Casey Stengel was the only man in baseball who could talk to all the people and make everybody feel the same. He made everybody feel good. He made everybody feel special.

It didn't matter who it was. He talked to the president of the United States and the president of General Motors. He talked to the guy driving the jackhammer and the guy driving the truck, the lawyer and the prisoner, the painter, the electrician, the priest, the rabbi, the guy selling peanuts in the park, the writer covering the game, and the poor man walking down the street who couldn't afford a ticket to the game.

It didn't matter to Casey. He made time for everybody. He never wasted time trying to figure out who you were. He talked to kings and he talked to hobos. He was the manager of some of the greatest baseball teams in history. And yet he had time for everybody.

Casey Stengel was every person's person. Casey Stengel was America. Nothing more. Nothing less.

He was the farmer plowing the field. He was the guy painting the silo. He was the cop walking the beat. He was the plumber, the banker, the lawyer. He represented everybody.

Casey knew his baseball. He only made it look like he was fooling around. The Old Man was one of the wisest men ever to step across that foul line. He knew every move that was ever invented and some that we haven't even caught on to yet.

He knew the game inside and out. He knew the game like John McGraw, Connie Mack, Miller Huggins, and all the great ones. He was smart as a fox. He invented the platoon system. Now we all use it.

Did you ever check all the players he picked up for the Yankees in July or August when they needed someone to push themselves over the top? Every one of them contributed to a pennant. It was amazing; he was never wrong. That ain't luck.

Casey went beyond the baseball mechanics, though. He added that special touch. Being around him was like Christmas every day. He broke baseball right down to its bones. Baseball is supposed to be fun. That's what Casey made it.

Baseball is nothing but a bunch of grown-up kids doing the same thing they did on the playgrounds when they were in school. Even in the big leagues, that's all it is.

Baseball hasn't changed. That's one of its beauties. It's still sixty feet and six inches from the pitcher's mound to home plate. It's still ninety feet to each base. Nine innings. No clock. Four balls, we get a free base. Three strikes, we sit down and wait till next time. The pitcher tries to throw the ball past the batter. The batter tries to hit it out of the park.

Baseball doesn't change from the first time we play in the sandlots till the last game we play as a pro. I hope it never does. Somewhere along the way though, most of us lose that childhood magic. For whatever reason, we try to make baseball a grown-up game.

Casey never did. He would never allow it. He loved baseball too much. He knew that baseball is all about having fun and never losing the kid inside. He knew that once we lose the kid, we lose it all.

Casey Stengel managed in the major leagues when he was seventy-six years old. And not for a minute did he ever lose the kid inside him. He knew it was all for fun. He tried to share that fun with everyone around him. He knew inside he still was a kid. That was the difference between Casey and all the other managers, even the great ones. Casey was a kid for life.

I've been lucky. I've gone against two of the greatest managers in history—Gene Mauch and Walter Alston. Alston is in the Hall of Fame and Mauch is a lead-pipe cinch to make it. Both contributed greatly to the game. As good as they were though, they didn't have that special something. They didn't have Casey's magic touch.

Casey knew that baseball is a show. He knew the stage belonged to him. He knew that nobody could play it better than he could. He was Bob Hope and Jack Benny rolled into one. On the field and off, The Old Man knew he had to perform. When he walked into Yankee Stadium and saw fifty thousand people packed in—

Casey was on stage. Those people were his audience. He loved to play the audience because he knew them so well.

That's the message Casey was trying to tell all of us. Every time we put on that uniform, we are on stage. We have to perform. People are paying their hard-earned money to see us perform. We've got to give them the best we've got every time we go out there. That's show business.

Casey could have played Broadway every night for thirty straight years without ever giving a bad performance. He wouldn't stand for it. That's the highest compliment I can give the man.

How can anyone ever come close to that? It's impossible.

Casey had that special style about him. He never called a player by his name. He'd say: "I'm going to tell you about my center fielder" or "that guy who's hitting third in my lineup."

"That guy hitting third" only happened to be Mickey Mantle!

It didn't matter. Casey knew who he was talking about. It was all part of the game he played. He knew every player. He knew everything about each and every one. It was just his way of having some fun, and it sure gave the writers something to write about.

He was beautiful when he talked. He used some of the funniest words. I'm sure he made some up. He'd drop them into the middle of a sentence when you didn't know what to expect. By the time you figured out what he'd said, he was already telling another story. He'd start telling the writers one story and right in the middle, he'd switch to another. Before finishing either of those, he might start a third. When he thought he had everyone confused, he'd jump right back and finish the first one he'd started.

That was no accident. It was all by design. He loved to fool around with people. That was his game plan. He was so sharp, he knew how to confuse you and throw you off track. He had a very powerful mind. It looked like he was wandering, but he was in control all the time.

I was at the New York Baseball Writers Dinner in January 1972. The writers had voted to give me the Mr. Nice Guy Award. I was honored just to be there, but it became a very special occasion for me because I got to sit next to Casey. It had been fifteen years since Don Larsen pitched a perfect game in the World Series, so the writers were going to honor Larsen with a special award, and they'd asked Casey to present it.

Casey was dressed in a tux. He was beautiful. The hotel ballroom was filled with all kinds of former Yankee greats and other baseball dignitaries and writers.

It really was a special occasion and, of course, Casey made the most of the moment. When he was introduced and asked to come on stage to present the award, the place went absolutely crazy. You would have thought the Pope had come into the room.

Casey took the microphone and started to talk about Larsen and what kind of mark he left on baseball by pitching that perfect game. He was going on and on when he spotted Billy Martin sitting in the audience. That triggered Casey and now he was on a roll.

Casey started to talk about "Billy the Kid"—"that spark plug from Berkeley, California." Casey carried on about how Billy was a battler and that if ever there was a fight, you could find Billy smack in the middle of it. Casey liked Martin because Billy was just a little guy who played as hard as he could. I think Billy represented the everyday workingman to Casey.

Just when everyone thought he was finished talking, Casey switched gears and started to ramble about Frankie Frisch.

"Now when you talk about Yankee second basemen," Casey said "you can't forget Frisch. He ran around all over that field. He went diving to his left . . . diving to his right. He slid into bases harder than a brick wall falling down."

When he finally finished with Frisch the crowd was roaring. It was wild. Casey had them in the palm of his hand and played it all the way.

Right in the middle of his routine, Casey waved to the

crowd. He walked off the stage and sat down next to me at the table.

The award for Larsen was still at the podium and Larsen was still sitting at his table laughing at Casey's stories. He probably forgot he was supposed to go up on the stage.

Phil Pepe, a baseball writer in New York, was master of ceremonies. Pepe went to the microphone, called Larsen to the stage and presented him the award.

A lot of people thought Casey plain forgot to give Larsen the award. He didn't forget. He knew all along exactly what he was doing.

Casey made all those people laugh before he sat down. He knew that doing it this way would leave an impact. People would remember that award for a long time. I know I have.

I was fortunate to be with Casey on several other occasions. My wife, Carol, was with us once at a fancy dinner for charity. I wore a tux with a tail. We were honored to sit at Casey's table.

During the night Casey told a hundred different stories. They all seemed to run together. But they all made a point.

"I don't know why people say they can't understand him," Carol said. "If you listen to him carefully, everything makes sense. He makes everything sound so simple. But he's very wise."

That was Casey's brilliance. He made the profound sound simple and the simple so profound. He twisted and turned to throw you off track. But if you stuck with him, there was a slice of wisdom in every story.

The Old Man was a genius. He owned banks. He could have been successful in whatever field he chose because he knew people and how to play the game. He just happened to pick baseball.

Casey became a very wealthy man. But you wouldn't have known he had a dime. He never tried to show he was a big shot. He treated everybody the same. He treated them the way he expected to be treated. He never asked for anything special.

Casey loved people. He loved everybody. He loved his players.

He loved the fans. He loved the rich people he met and he loved the people who were too poor even to buy a ticket for the game. Casey didn't know how to separate them. He couldn't love somebody more just because he happened to be wealthy.

For every World Series, each manager, player, and coach gets the opportunity to buy a certain number of tickets for family and friends. The manager's tickets are usually some of the best in the house. Everyone wants them.

Casey made sure to take care of his family with tickets. But you never knew who else might show up in his seats.

Casey bought them and then gave them to certain people who might never get the chance to see a World Series game. They weren't necessarily high-powered businessmen. Casey might give them to the bellhop at the hotel or the waitress in the coffee shop. If he liked you and started talking to you, it didn't matter what you did or where you came from. You were his friend and he wanted to take care of you.

I won't lie. I'm aware of the comparisons between Casey and me. Of course, I'm honored. That's the highest compliment anyone could ever give me.

I'm not trying to sound modest. I'm only telling the truth. I can't be compared to The Old Man. Nobody can. I appreciate the compliment, but comparing anyone to Casey is a sacrilege.

Casey Stengel, the legend, will always be with us. He's here for eternity. I might pass him in actual number of wins. But I won't ever catch him for what he meant to the game. Nobody will. Yet he's the man I must chase. The closer I get to him, the more I've contributed to the game.

I share with The Old Man my love for people. I'm proud of all the titles and awards I've won. As Casey once said, "They're in the book . . . you can look them up." Yet those are just awards and numbers. I'm prouder of my love for people. Fans are what make the game. They're the most important thing to me. It was the same for Casey. It was all about the show.

That's why I enjoy spring training so much. In spring training we don't play in fifty-thousand-seat stadiums. There are five or six thousand people. I can wave to the fans, talk with them, reach out and touch them. For that moment, they become part of the game.

Nobody cares if we win or lose in Florida. All the people care about is having a little fun. They want to see the players up close. They want to talk to them. It's my job to make them feel good. I want to make them feel part of it. It's the show and I've got to give them the very best I can.

Casey did it. The Old Man used to take all the fun of spring training and run it through the season for the next six months. He had to be very special to pull that off.

Very few managers know how to enjoy the game the way Casey did. He enjoyed every single minute. If we look at managing a baseball team as a job, we're wrong. We are in the wrong business. We ought to pick up a paintbrush or a license to drive a truck.

This is not a job. This is fun. Our only job is to make sure that we share that fun with the fans. This is show business. That's why, to me, nobody will ever top Casey Stengel. Not Babe Ruth. Not Ty Cobb. Not Lou Gehrig. Not Joe DiMaggio. Not Reggie Jackson. Not Pete Rose. Nobody could play the game like Casey.

Casey Stengel made people smile. He made people want to be around him. What a tremendous gift to make people want to be by your side.

The Old Man is still around. This might sound silly, but I believe The Old Man looks at us every day and says, "Come on and get me. Get with the show."

That's Casey Stengel. He'll live forever. Casey Stengel was baseball. He was the show. In my mind, he still is.

The World Series

There ain't a kid alive in this country who doesn't dream about playing in the World Series. He might dream about hitting the home run in extra innings to win it all. He might dream about pitching the seventh game. I spent my first nine years in Bridgewater, South Dakota, and I know even out there I dreamed about it an awful lot.

As a kid, the World Series always seemed to be between the Yankees and Dodgers. In fact, I thought there never was a World Series without the Yankees and Dodgers. I can't remember any of the other ones.

Even in my wildest dreams I never thought I'd actually be in one. I never got to play in one. But I've been very lucky to manage in five of them and win the last three.

All the dreams I ever had about being in a World Series—all the anticipation, all the fears, all the excitement—all those tingling anxieties don't mean a thing until you've been there. Because until you have, you can't even imagine how much greater all those feelings really become.

My first World Series was 1970. I was the thirty-six-year-old first-year manager of the Cincinnati Reds and we played the Baltimore Orioles. I'm not ashamed to admit that I was so awed by all the dreams I had about the World Series and all the media, hype, and happenings that go along with actually being in it that I spent my whole time watching and trying to comprehend exactly what the heck was going on. I cannot truly remember much about the 1970 World Series except for Brooks Robinson making all those great plays at third base. Every time I looked up there was Brooksie diving here and diving there to squelch a rally. On top of that, he came up with a big hit every time he had the opportunity.

People don't realize how the whole thing engulfs you the first time you're in it. Your whole life is simply taken over. From the moment your team comes to town, your life no longer belongs to you. The whole world takes a little piece of it.

A truckload of television cameras are waiting for you at the airport. Writers seem to come out from every crack in the pavement. They're at the airport. They're at the park. They're at the hotel, which is packed. It's like New Year's Eve at Times Square. There must be a thousand writers everywhere you go. You wonder who's putting out the papers because everybody seems to be around.

When you come down for breakfast, the hotel already is packed with people and the writers are waiting. It's the same thing for lunch and the same thing for dinner. They had my head spinning so fast I didn't know where I was.

They say the first World Series is the one you remember most.

No, no, no! I guarantee you don't remember that one because that fantasy world you always dreamed about is suddenly real. And the thing has ten thousand legs and it simply eats you up.

If you're fortunate to go back again, you know what to expect ahead of time. If you're smart, you know just about how every day is going to roll. You know how to attack it.

The first thing you do is to cut off your phone. If I have to talk to somebody, I call them. You don't go through the lobby of the hotel for breakfast, lunch, or dinner. If you want to go out for dinner, you case out the hotel ahead of time so that you can sneak out the back door.

You learn how to deal with the horde of media people. Go to the park early. Get all interviews out of the way and then go out to the outfield for batting practice to clear your mind for the game. You have to learn these tricks so you can focus all your mental energy on the game. Because there's one trap you don't want to fall into and this thirty-six-year-old rookie manager fell into it face first.

The biggest mistake a manager can make is to think that because his team made it to the World Series the season was a success. There's no question that if your team made it to the Series it must have done something right during the regular season and the playoffs. There's no question that merely by participating, you experience the thrill of a lifetime. For ten days the eyes of the world are focused on you. With all the media, you get the chance to express your thoughts and feelings on a lot of things other than baseball.

That's all marvelous. But don't think that just because you made it to the World Series it doesn't matter who wins and who loses. That's the biggest mistake a manager can make. You better not lose.

When you lose a World Series, all the people around the country who have pulled so hard for you all year long become very bitter. They're happy that you've made it. And they pull hard for you throughout the whole affair. But if you lose it, you've let a lot of people down.

You must remember you represent every fan that club has. They've put their hearts and souls into this thing. Now you not only have a responsibility to yourself, your organization, your coaches, and your players but you also have a tremendous responsibility to all those fans. You owe them a victory so that they can gloat for the next six months. Anything less and those people must endure the embarrassment that their club lost.

That's an awesome responsibility. But I love the opportunity to play in that show.

1970—CINCINNATI VS. BALTIMORE

I was thirty-six years old managing in my first World Series and had absolutely no idea of what the heck was going on. To top all that, though, I started the affair with a couple of strikes against me. And I had no one to blame except myself.

The first strike came way back at the start of spring training when I boldly predicted that we'd win our division by ten games. We actually won by thirteen and a half, but that was one of the dumbest things I ever pulled in my life. I put a lot of pressure on my team and a lot of pressure on myself. I could have the world's greatest All-Star Team and never again would I say something so ridiculous.

What the heck was I thinking about?

We won seventy of our first hundred games and cruised into the playoffs against the Pittsburgh Pirates.

The Pirates had some ferocious hitters like Willie Stargell, Roberto Clemente, Manny Sanguillen, Al Oliver, and Richie Hebner. Deep in my heart, I thought they might have the better team. But we beat them three straight games and were headed to the World Series against the Baltimore Orioles.

That's where I made another deadly mistake. Like everyone who had been brought up in the National League, I thought that the National League was far superior to the American. I felt we had already beaten the best club in baseball and now we were going to show Baltimore what the game was all about. I thought we were going to roll over the Orioles.

I look back now and wonder what planet I was on.

There's no question Baltimore had the better club. They had better pitching. We had no pitching at all.

Jim Merritt won twenty games for us during the season. He had a sore elbow and pitched just 1²/₃ innings. Jim McGlothlin was hurt and pitched only 4²/₃ innings. Wayne Simpson had a sore shoulder and couldn't pitch at all. Those were three main starters and all of them were hurt. We didn't have a chance.

Without a doubt, Baltimore was the best club because they had sound pitching and were totally healthy. They had Jim Palmer, Mike Cuellar, and Dave McNally. All three were twenty-game winners.

All I can remember is Robinson making all those great plays. I have the film at home. I don't even watch it anymore. I don't care to see it. I don't want to know about it. Baltimore was the best team.

That Series didn't do anything other than wake me up and make me realize that I had let a lot of people down. Fortunately, I don't remember enough of it for it to bother me. But it sure woke me up for the next time. I knew I had an enormous responsibility.

1972—CINCINNATI VS. OAKLAND

Everybody says that the Cincinnati–Boston World Series of 1975 was the best in history.

I don't. I'll always maintain that the best Series I was ever in was the 1972 Series against Oakland. That's because those were the two finest clubs to go against each other you'll ever see in I don't know how long.

But I managed to put my foot in my mouth once again before

the Series even got started. Before the opening game some of the writers asked how I felt about the Series.

"Cincinnati and Pittsburgh are the two best teams in baseball," I said. "We beat the Pirates in the National League Playoffs. That sort of makes the World Series anticlimactic."

Was I nuts? I had to be. I felt in my heart what I said was true. But it was flat-out suicidal to say something like that about a World Series opponent.

The Oakland A's were a far better team than I had given them credit for. They proved that where it counted—on the field. They whipped us fair and square.

It was the perfect match. Six of the seven games were decided by one run. There were more good plays in that Series than you'll ever see in a whole season. Everybody rose to the occasion. It was picture-perfect baseball.

Oakland was much better than the 1970 Baltimore team that beat us. Oakland was an outstanding team. In fact, Oakland was the best team I ever managed against. Without a doubt, the Cincinnati teams I managed were the best clubs. But Oakland was the best I went up against. They proved it. They won three straight World Series.

We should have won in 1972. I blew the Series.

We dropped the first two games at Cincinnati. Joe Rudi killed us in left field. He made plays Harry Houdini couldn't have made to beat us in two games we should have won.

We went out to Oakland and shut them out, 1–0. We had Game Four won in the ninth. Then I blew it with a decision I should never have made.

We had a 2–1 lead going into the bottom of the ninth with Clay Carroll on the mound. Up stepped a pinch hitter named Gonzalo Marquez. We had gone over all of their players and knew where to play them defensively. Ray Shore, our advance scout, said that every ball Marquez hit in the air went to left field. Shore said that if he hit the ball on the ground, he went up the middle. He did not pull it into the hole at short.

Our shortstop, David Concepcion, knew Marquez well from Venezuela. Concepcion told me that Marquez hit everything toward the left side. So I went over Shore's advice and played David over in the hole. Sure enough, Marquez hit a high bouncing ball up the middle. Concepcion stopped it but couldn't make the play. Had he been up the middle where I should have had him, it would have been a routine out and we would have had them.

The A's came up with three more singles to push across two runs and we were down, three games to one.

After the game Shore came into my office visibly upset. He picked up the little red scouting book from my desk. He started to thumb through the pages. He didn't have to. I know what he was looking for. He slammed the book down and walked out of the room.

Shore told me off later in private. He had a right to and I accepted his criticism.

We both agreed that crying over it wouldn't bring back the game. But I learned my lesson. Ray Shore is a fantastic scout. I never went against his suggestions again.

We bounced back to beat them the next day and then trounced them the first day back in Cincinnati to even it at three games apiece.

That Series was destined to be the A's because in the seventh game they came up with plays like I never saw before. Hal McRae hit a bases-loaded shot that would have scored three runs for us, but their center fielder, Angel Mangual, made a miraculous catch to stop a big rally. Then with a runner on third, Gene Tenace hit a grounder right at our third baseman. It hit the seam of the artificial turf and bounced up into left field for a run.

That's the way things went. Oakland deserved to win. I'll never take anything away from that great team. But there's no way to this day that anyone will tell me that the Oakland baseball team was better than Cincinnati.

SPARKY!

That was a tremendous World Series. I don't believe we'll ever
see another one played that well by the two best teams in baseball for a particular year. But I still think I blew it in Game Four
when I didn't station Concepcion where I should have.

1975—CINCINNATI VS. BOSTON

Many people think this was the greatest World Series that was
ever played. It was a tremendous Series. There was a lot of drama
and a lot of color to it.

There were also a lot of outstanding plays. As I said, though,
there never will be another World Series with as much crisp
baseball as the one in 1972.

I don't want to take anything away from the 1975 Series,
especially because I came up with my first win. It was tremendous more for the excitement we generated for the country than
for the actual baseball play itself.

So much attention was focused on that Series because after we
took a three games to two lead heading back to Boston, we ran
into a New England storm that simply refused to die.

We had the usual travel day after Game Five. Then the storms
just hung over all of New England for three more days. We had a
four-day layoff before getting to Game Six.

The media coverage was overwhelming. We not only got all
the attention from all the sports reporters, but now all the
nightly news shows got into the act.

The buildup for Game Six was unbelievable. It became an
event bigger than the World Series. And all the drama for twelve
innings made it one of the single most remembered games in
history.

There were several good plays. In the ninth inning, George
Foster made a do-or-die throw for us to cut down Denny Doyle at
the plate with what would have been the winning run.

In the eleventh Joe Morgan was robbed of a home run by right fielder Dwight Evans.

The play that turned it all around, though, came in the eighth inning. And I felt like I almost blew the whole Series again because of a decision I didn't make.

We had a 6–3 lead with two out in the eighth. Boston sent Bernie Carbo up to pinch hit with two men on. Carbo was a left-handed hitter. I had Rawly Eastwick, a right-hander, pitching. I had Will McEnaney, a lefty, warming up and ready in the bullpen.

Eastwick got two strikes on Carbo. All I had to do was go out right then and bring in McEnaney. With that big left-handed curve coming from Port Arthur, I'm convinced he would have struck out Carbo.

I was all set to make the move. I took one step up the dugout steps. Then for a reason I simply do not know, I changed my mind. I stopped, spun around, and got back in the dugout.

I had him right where I wanted him and suddenly I changed my mind. I had never done that before and I've never done it since.

Carbo hit the three-run homer to tie it and then Carlton Fisk won it with that dramatic home run down the left field line in the twelfth.

It was a stupid mistake. I made a stupid mistake then and I made one in the 1972 Series. I'm not ashamed of them. I made them and I admit that. To me, if you admit your mistakes, you don't have a problem dealing with yourself.

After the game was one of the low points of my life. I couldn't believe what had happened. I was young then and the only thing that kept running through my mind was that I cost us two World Series. Here I was, manager of the Big Red Machine, and we couldn't win the big one. I thought everyone would think we were like the Dallas Cowboys. We were always good enough to get there but not good enough to put it away.

I'll never forget walking to the bus after that game. Pete Rose came up to me.

"You know what?" he said. "That's the greatest baseball game I ever played in."

I stared at him. My face must have been blank.

"Peter Edward, how can you say that's the greatest game when we had it won and I blew it?" I asked.

He looked at me. His face was hard as a rock.

"I'll tell you why," he said. "Because people will be talking about that game for years to come.

"This is going to be history tomorrow. It's going to be really something. We're going to win. I promise you a victory. There's no way Boston can beat us tomorrow."

I felt pretty good about what Rose had said. But when I got back to the hotel I was still nervous. I had two beds in my room. I asked Ray Shore to come up because I couldn't go to sleep. We sat and talked till about four in the morning. Finally I told Ray I was going to sleep.

It didn't last long. We were up at seven-thirty. Ray asked me to go down to the press room for breakfast.

"Are you kidding?" I said. "There ain't no way I'm going anywhere near the media now."

He begged me. He told me it would help to get my mind off things. Finally I agreed.

I stayed in that press room all morning and all afternoon till it was time to go to the park. I told story after story and we all were laughing. When I got to the park, I was the most relaxed man in the world. I didn't know how we were going to win it. I didn't care. But somehow I just knew we were going to take this thing. This was going to be my first world championship. I truly believed it.

We were tied 3–3 going into the ninth. And wouldn't you know that it was a Joe Morgan single that won the game.

1976—CINCINNATI VS. NEW YORK

I never had any doubt about this one. The Big Red Machine was at its peak. When all is said and done and all the history books

about baseball are written, that 1976 Reds team will rate with
the 1927 Yankees.

After the first game I passed Si Burick in the runway coming
up from the dugout.

"Cyrus, don't say a thing," I whispered to him. "But this thing
is going to end in four games. The Yankees cannot beat us."

I wasn't bragging. That's actually the kind of talent we had.
The Yankees had a good team. But they didn't have anything like
we did. We were so good and so strong.

Our 1976 club is the only team in history that's ever swept the
playoffs and the World Series. I don't believe anyone will ever do
that again.

We won 108 games in the regular season, then 7 straight in the
playoffs and World Series. That's a 169-game season and we won
115 times. Even more incredible was a statistic from the regular
season. Our regular eight starters—Johnny Bench, Tony Perez,
Joe Morgan, Dave Concepcion, Pete Rose, George Foster, Cesar
Geronimo, and Ken Griffey—were in the starting lineup as a
unit only fifty-six times.

Now to top even that, our record in those games was 48–8!

I just believed in resting regulars when I had the chance. And
all they did was keep on winning.

They were so good they actually toyed with people. It was like
a cat and mouse in a cartoon.

If you wanted to play a power game, we'd stand still and play
all the power you wanted. If you wanted to open it up with a
speed game, we'd start running. We stole over two hundred
bases and were safe on 84 percent of our attempts.

We played whatever type of game you wanted to play. That's
the last truly great team we've seen in baseball. I'll never again
see another team come close to it. There was nothing on the face
of the earth in a baseball uniform better than what I walked into
Yankee Stadium with.

Playing at Yankee Stadium was a special thrill because I had
never been there before. It was a tremendous feeling. I was awed
to think that this is where Ruth and Gehrig and DiMaggio and

Mantle and Berra and all those legends played. But I was not awed by the Yankees. I knew we were the baddest cats.

The one thing that disappointed me about the 1976 Series was the incident involving Thurman Munson. I love Thurman Munson. But there was a terrible mistake. And it wasn't made by me. Something I said was twisted by the media and an incident was created when there shouldn't have been one at all.

Munson hit over .500 for the Series. But he did just what we wanted him to do. We made up our minds before the Series started that we were going to let him hit all the singles to right field that he wanted. But we refused to let him hit for power. We pitched him so that he had to hit the ball to right field all day long. We allowed him all the ground ball singles he could get. But we weren't going to let him hurt us.

At a press conference the media asked me to compare Munson with Johnny Bench. I remember exactly what I said.

"Please, do not ever embarrass Johnny Bench or any other catcher by trying to compare him to Bench. There ain't anyone even close to him."

I said that then and I'll say it now. There'll never be anyone who will come close to Bench. I never said a single detrimental word about Munson. In fact, he was sitting directly to my right at the press conference. But when they wrote about it, they twisted my words around and created a controversy that never should have been.

I wrote Thurman Munson a letter explaining everything. I mailed it to him at Yankee Stadium. I never said that Thurman Munson was not a great catcher. But neither Thurman Munson nor any other catcher was ever a Johnny Bench. There will never be another one like Johnny Bench.

Bench had an off year in 1976, batting a career low .234 with 16 home runs and 74 RBI. When it counted in the Series, though, Bench came to play.

After batting .333 in the National League Playoffs, he went eight for fifteen in the Series and knocked in six runs in the four games.

When it was all over, John said that the Reds had carried him all season . . . now he was just giving something back.

He sure did.

1984—DETROIT VS. SAN DIEGO

We split the two games in San Diego. After we won the first game at Detroit, I thought the Series was won. I remember saying to myself, "We're going to end it here. We won't have to go back to San Diego."

Fortunately I was right. I wanted to win that Series so badly. The Tiger franchise has been so good to baseball for so many years. It deserved a victory. The players deserved a victory because they were such a close group. Everyone knew his role and everyone accepted it. When it came down to a tight situation everyone delivered.

I had a personal stake in it, too. I won't lie. I had just become the first manager ever to win 100 games in a season with two different teams. I wanted to become the first manager ever to win a Series in both leagues. But the big thing was winning for the players and for the fans. Detroit fans are the best in the country regardless of the sport.

We took the Series in five games. We had swept the playoffs from Kansas City. And we won a club record 104 games during the regular season.

In the eighth inning of Game Five at Detroit, Kirk Gibson capped the most magical season in Tiger history by drilling his second home run of the game. It was a mammoth blast way up into the right field upper deck off Goose Gossage with runners on second and third.

I didn't think the Padres were going to pitch to him with first base open. In fact, neither did San Diego Manager Dick Williams. Williams had held up four fingers indicating he wanted to intentionally walk Gibson. I held up four fingers and yelled to Gibby, "They don't want to pitch to you!"

But Gossage called Williams to the mound and talked him into letting him pitch to Gibby.

Gibson looked over at me in the dugout and held up all ten fingers. He bet me $10 that not only would they pitch to him, but that he would hit a home run.

Gibby won his bet and put the whole state of Michigan into a state of frenzy. As he circled the bases with both arms extended, I couldn't believe that 1984 finally was coming to a close with the big prize in the garage.

But it was one of the most difficult seasons I ever experienced in my whole life.

We won our first nine games. One of them was a no-hitter by Jack Morris at Chicago. The most amazing thing about that season and one of the most amazing things of any season in history was that after our first forty games we were 35–5!

That's incredible. Even a super sandlot team doesn't go 35–5. Not in baseball. There are too many things that can go wrong. I kept pinching myself to make sure I wasn't dreaming.

I remember the night we made it to 35–5. We had just taken our third straight game against the Angels at Anaheim. We got on the team bus heading for the airport to fly to Seattle.

"We ought to make a stop in Las Vegas on the way," I said to one of the coaches sitting next to me.

I wasn't trying to act smart. In fact, I was somewhat in a daze. I honestly wasn't convinced this was real.

We were setting record after record. Most wins at the start of a season. Most consecutive wins on the road. Media from all over the country followed our every move. It became like a playoff atmosphere even before we got to June. We were like the freak at a carnival. Everyone wanted to see us. Nobody goes 35–5.

I was brought down to earth for a moment during our first trip to Anaheim. I was sitting with my wife in the hotel coffee shop. I was smoking my pipe when a man walked up to our table. I thought he was going to ask me to stop smoking.

"Aren't you Sparky Anderson?" he asked.

I told him I was. He said he was originally from Ohio. He told me how much he admired me when I managed at Cincinnati.

"By the way . . . what are you doing now?" he asked.

He wasn't being a wise guy. He was dead serious. That's when reality smacked me right in the kisser. Here we were 35–5, setting record after record, and this old fan of mine wanted to know what I was doing now.

It was a good lesson. I knew how quickly things could turn around.

In fact, that's what scared me most. I was uneasy the whole year. I worried like I never did before. I'll never do that again. I won't put myself through that. It wasn't a fun season.

I worried because we had no right to go 35–5. No team has that right. We had taken our fans to a height they had never been before. If we had let them down, there would have been serious depression. On top of that, we would have gone down as one of the biggest chokes in history. I would have had to live with that for the rest of my life. That wasn't an easy feeling.

We had a marvelous club. On paper against some other teams, though, we came up a little short. Our top two players were Alan Trammell and Lou Whitaker. We also had Lance Parrish, Kirk Gibson, Darrell Evans, and Chet Lemon. Those were our six key players.

Our starting staff was Jack Morris, Dan Petry, and Milt Wilcox. We ran five other starters out for the last two spots. In the bullpen, Willie Hernandez had a make-believe season. He saved thirty-three games in thirty-four opportunities. He had two great set-up men in Aurelio Lopez and Doug Bair.

The whole season was a fairy tale. Every time we needed a big hit in the ninth inning someone would come up with a double. Players like Dave Bergman and Rusty Kuntz and Marty Castillo did things no one thought they were capable of, and it kept happening all year long. They played with such great enthusiasm. Whenever they had to win, they won.

One of the keys was the fact that everyone got a fair share of playing time. When certain players weren't in the lineup, they were pulling for their teammates and ready to jump into action if needed. It was a very close group. Calling a team "family" is an overused expression. But that's as close to a family as I've ever seen a baseball club.

Everyone thought we cruised through the season. But there were two or three times when we could have lost everything. There was a point in August when we lost four straight games to Kansas City, including a Sunday doubleheader. We had to go to Boston to play five games in three days.

All I wanted were two wins in Boston. We got them and left town with the seven game lead we went in with.

We were finished with doubleheaders for the rest of the year. I knew with our staff that we could have at least three strong starters out of every five days the rest of the way.

We won going away. After we swept Kansas City in the play-offs, I had no question in my mind we would win the World Series.

Roger Craig was my pitching coach. After the Series he was over for a barbecue.

"If the public only knew what you and I know," Roger said, "then they'd know why you worried so much. This was a miracle."

It was a very good team. They played so hard. But we had no business going 35–5 or winning 104 games.

I have a sign on the wall in my office—Always Believe in Miracles. If you believe long enough, a miracle will happen. That certainly was one.

Kids will always dream about playing in the World Series. I'll go on with my dreams, too.

I'd love to manage a couple more. There's no other feeling in sports that can match it. Nothing comes close.

The World Series is magic.

Fired!

There's an old saying in baseball that a manager is hired only to be fired. That gets proven year after year. Some of the guys get recycled like returnable bottles. They get fired in one city and simply move on to the next. It's like musical chairs.

That's the way baseball goes. Clubs can't fire all their players so the manager is the first to go. It's been like that since the game began.

I never really thought anything like that could happen to me. Not to Sparky. Not to the manager of The Big Red Machine.

I was shot down to earth on November 27, 1978. That's the day I was fired from the Cincinnati Reds.

It's hard to believe that was almost twelve years ago. It's hard to believe all the things that have happened since then. When it happened I was totally shocked. I had no idea. It was like one of those monsters that jump out of nowhere in some dark haunted-house ride in an amusement park.

After the season, I went with the Reds on an exhibition tour to Japan. It was a marvelous experience. We played several games there and were treated like royalty everywhere we went.

Dick Wagner was general manager of the Reds back then. He was in Japan for a few games but had to leave early. At the time, Tommy John and Lee Lacy were free agents. We had some interest in them and he went back to see about signing them. We didn't sign either one, but Dick made an effort.

The rest of us flew back together. We flew all night long and got back to Cincinnati at four o'clock in the afternoon on a Wednesday. We were really tired. I checked my daughter, Shirlee, into the Holiday Inn. We were flying home to Los Angeles later that day.

I immediately went to the ballpark to see Dick. There had been some disagreements between me and the front office about the coaching staff for next year. They wanted to make a change. I didn't. I won't say who was involved because it wouldn't be fair to either side. That was a good thing about dealing with Wagner. When it came to matters like this, what was said between him and me stayed right there. I never worried that he would tell stories out of school about me and he never worried about me. I may talk a lot, but I never break a promise of silence. We agreed never to mention names and to my knowledge we never have. There's no sense in embarrassing anyone.

They wanted some guys out. I didn't. We had talked about the matter when we were in San Francisco in August. I wouldn't budge.

They didn't say yes or no to me. They told me we'd settle it in Japan. We didn't. I thought we could settle it when I went home.

When I got to Dick's office I saw his desk was full. He was

really busy. He said he'd been away so long that things really got stacked up.

"Can I call you Monday?" Wagner asked me.

I told him of course.

"Will you be home?" he asked.

"I'll be home if you tell me you're going to call," I answered. "But I want to get this coaching thing cleared up. You know I want them all back."

I went home to Thousand Oaks. Sunday night I got a call from Wagner. He asked if I could meet him Monday morning at the Marriott Hotel in the Los Angeles airport.

I got there at nine o'clock. I called his room and he said he'd be right down. He told me to get a table for breakfast. I thought he had Lacy locked up and he was there to see what I thought about making the deal.

"Have airplane will travel," I joked with him when he walked into the restaurant.

At breakfast we talked about a lot of little things, mostly about the trip to Japan.

It was ten o'clock when we finished and he asked me up to his room. It was room 1118. I'll never forget it. Every time my wife and I drive by the airport, I point toward that room.

"There it is—1118," I say. "That's where the ax fell."

As soon as we walked into the room, Dick went into the bathroom. I went over to a big, old, soft chair and sank into it. At that time I smoked cigarettes. I lit one, put my feet up on a stool and was as comfortable as a king. I really wasn't thinking about anything when Dick came out of the bathroom. He didn't say a word. He just walked up and stood in front of me.

"I have something very tough to do," he said. "We're not going to bring you back."

I heard what he said, but it didn't sink in. I sat there trying to put his words together. I knew what they meant but they didn't make sense.

After a couple of moments he sat down and went over the

coaching staff. He told me which ones were coming back and which ones weren't. Then he asked me about some of the other members of the staff. He asked me what I thought about the trainer, the clubhouse manager, and the traveling secretary. I told him I thought all of them did outstanding jobs.

Then he hit me with something funny.

"We have to pay you for next year so we'd like you to do some special assignment scouting if we call on you," he said.

I remained perfectly calm. I was polite but I was as direct as I could be.

"Oh no," I said. "You're paying me because you have to. My contract says you're paying me to manage. That's the only thing it says. So don't be calling on me to do no scouting."

He listened and he understood.

"Can I ask you a favor then?" he said. "We plan to announce this at eleven A.M. Cincinnati time tomorrow. Will you please not say a word to the press about it until then?"

"You have my word on that," I told him.

There was another pause. He wanted another promise.

"If you go to the winter meetings or if anybody calls you, would you please not make any comments at all about our players?" he said.

I couldn't go along with that.

"I can't make you that promise, Dick," I said. "That wouldn't be fair. As far as I'm concerned, I no longer work for you. If anyone calls me on a player, I'll give them my honest opinion. You don't have my word on that one."

He understood again. Finally he stood up and was crying. He hugged me. Real hard.

I turned around, walked out the door, and never looked back. That was it. I was history.

I'm not sure what went through my mind when I got into the car. I remember turning on the radio, half-thinking I'd hear something about me getting fired. Every station was running a special report on the mayor of San Francisco who got shot. It kept my mind off things. I remember thinking that I had just gotten fired, but this guy just got killed.

When I got home, nobody was there. My wife and oldest son, Lee, had gone out with a real estate lady to look at a house my son was interested in buying. I went across the street to see my friend Jack. He wasn't home either. I thought to myself—here I am fired and nobody is around.

When I went back home, my youngest son, Albert, was home from school eating lunch.

"Albert, I want to tell you something," I told him. "Daddy just got fired from the Reds."

He was sitting on the couch watching TV while he ate. He told me not to worry about it.

"I still love you, Daddy," he said.

Finally the rest of my family came home with the real estate lady. They were all excited because Lee and his wife liked the house they saw and wanted to make a deposit.

I wrote out a check for $1,000 and then the real estate lady left. My daughter, Shirlee, was going up to her room.

"Sissy, come here," I said, "All of you sit down. I've got something to tell you. I just got fired."

I thought I had been surprised; they were shocked frozen. I explained what had happened and told them none of us could say anything about it because I had given my word.

Somehow that night word leaked out back in Cincinnati about a big press conference scheduled for the next day. I got a call from Marty Brenneman, one of Cincinnati's radio announcers. He asked me what it was going to be about.

"I'm not one hundred percent sure, Marty," I said. "But I will tell you this. I wouldn't miss it if I were you."

A couple of writers called. I told them the same thing.

The next morning the story appeared in the Dayton paper. That's when all hell broke loose.

Wagner's secretary, Patty, called to apologize for what had happened and to warn me what to expect. I had two phone lines at the time and both of them started ringing like burglar alarms.

I got up a little after seven A.M. One of the first calls came from Joe Morgan. Joe was all worked up. He was really upset over the firing.

"Little man, let me tell you something," I told Joe. "I don't want you to say a bad word. If we're friends like I think we are, I don't want no bad words.

"You've got a new manager. Whether you like it or not, that man don't deserve to be greeted by what you have to say about me. We're friends. I have to ask you this favor. I don't want no defense on my behalf."

Joe still didn't like it. We had finished second with ninety-two wins. And we did it with more injuries to key players than you could count. He couldn't understand why this had to happen. We had a long talk and he said he'd honor my request.

I tried to get my mind off things so I went to the golf course. It didn't matter, though. The media found me. They came out to the course. There were writers, cameras, microphones.

When I got home, the phones were ringing off the hook. My wife was answering one and my daughter the other. They kept writing down names and numbers. The calls came from everywhere—Pacific time zone, Eastern time zone, Midwest time zone. They didn't stop until midnight when my wife switched the phones off.

I hadn't eaten anything all day. Carol made me some soup and then I went to bed.

I woke up at six o'clock the next morning. I went down to my den with the stack of messages. Albert got up early and came downstairs. I called him over.

"You sit here with Daddy," I told him. "I'm going to show you how to turn defeat into victory. I'm going to show you how you're supposed to act during the hardest times."

I think he learned something. It's easy to be gracious when everything is going for you. That's something even the village idiot can handle. When times get tough, you have to get a little tougher. Don't cry. Nobody cares about your problems. Everybody's got their own. Do your business and be a man.

Because of the time difference I started with all the calls from the East. I worked my way all across the country, returning every call. The first people I called were Pete Rose and Johnny Bench. They had called the night before. I told them pretty much what I had told Joe Morgan and that I was all right.

After I got done making all my calls, the phones started ringing again. Then TV cameras and writers started showing up at the door. I spent the whole day talking.

Over the next few days the mail poured in. The mailman couldn't believe it. Almost every letter said how sorry they were to see me go. They couldn't believe it happened. One of the Cincinnati papers ran a poll on the firing and I got 87 percent in favor of me staying.

It had never dawned on me that the people cared so much for me. I mean that. I really never had any inkling. I always thought it was for Rose and Bench and Morgan and all the rest of the Big Red Machine.

That's the way it should be. The players are supposed to be the heroes. I have to admit, though, it made me feel good.

For about the first month after I got fired, I don't think the reality of the situation really sank in. It was actually glamorous at first. It made me feel important. I was getting calls from everybody all over the country. Writers, TV stations, radio stations, magazines. I got all kinds of calls from people in baseball.

Two managers—Herman Franks and Bob Lemon—called. They tried to persuade me to go to the winter baseball meetings in Hollywood, Florida. I thanked them, but I refused. I couldn't go because I felt like I was on the outside looking in.

Coming off the career I had, I knew I would eventually get another job in baseball. But if I went to the meetings, all the other managers would have to talk to me. If they didn't, then I knew they had problems and were worried about their jobs. I didn't want to put anyone in that position.

Somebody told me that Whitey Herzog told all the other managers a story at the meetings.

"Boys, I got news for you," he said. "You better get off to a fast start next year because that cat with the white hair is sitting out there."

I asked Whitey about that later.

"Yeah, I said it," he told me. "And I made sure I was one of the guys who got off to a fast start."

After that first month, it finally hit me. It wouldn't be fair to say which ones, but I did get calls from six clubs that expressed an interest in me coming to manage. Detroit was not one that called at the time. Two clubs were very interested. I almost went to the one in the National League.

There was some speculation in the media about where I might be going, but it didn't get out of hand. No one really knew for sure which clubs were interested. I liked that because I would have felt awfully bad if someone who had a job felt that he was going to be replaced by me. They didn't need me breathing down their necks. I didn't talk to anyone about it and that's the way I feel business should be conducted. I wouldn't want anyone who did get a job that year to think he was the second choice because I had turned some team down.

It was good to know I was wanted. Then I realized none of that was important. What was important was that I had lost the place where I felt I should be. And I didn't think I had done anything to deserve that.

I refuse to make any excuses. I don't feel they're necessary. We won ninety-two games in 1978. We actually took the lead for a couple of days in early August. Then everybody started to get hurt. We had no one left at the end.

The last couple of months, our pitching staff came up with a series of little injuries that knocked things out of kilter just when we had them going.

The thing that really hurt were a couple of injuries to Bench and Morgan. These were two of my horses. Losing them together for a while was like throwing sand into our gas tank. Bench was down to 120 games that season. Morgan always wanted to be in the lineup and he was cut to 132.

I was confused over why I was fired. I couldn't understand why or how something like that could have happened to me. I'm not sure there was any one thing that led to it. Maybe it was just a case of being there so long. When you're at a place so long, both sides get irritated over little things that come up. Sometimes they build up and don't go away.

I suppose it's something like a marriage that goes bad. Nothing is ever one sided. I realize it was as much my fault as it was theirs. When you can admit that, then you can put it to rest. We were like a couple that lost our understanding of each other.

I don't mean just Dick Wagner and me. It wasn't Dick. All Dick did was carry out the job that was dictated by the front office.

Dick got the blame for it. In fact, the Cincinnati fans hung him in effigy down by the ballpark. He never cried about it. He took it like a man. That's why I respect him to this very day. We're still great friends. He knows that I know he was only doing his job.

Our friendship remains very tight. I still feel very close to the Reds. I especially have a warm feeling for their fans. They're tremendous.

As I look back, I think it was best for them and best for me. It was settled without a lot of bad talk. No bad talk from either side. It was a simple firing and it was over.

I honestly believe that if I had been willing to give up my staff, I probably could have saved my job. But there's no way in the world I would have let one of my people go. They weren't going out. Not for me. When things go wrong I don't think you can blame the coaching staff. If you want to blame anyone, blame me. That's the way I've always been. I pray to God that's the way I'll always be.

After the Tigers won the World Series in 1984, all the writers asked if I finally felt vindicated for being fired by Cincinnati. It wasn't a case of feeling vindicated. It never was. I never felt any hate for being fired. What bothered me was the fact that my coaches never got the credit they deserved.

When I managed the Reds I always used to joke with the writers.

"I can go to the Bahamas as long as my coaches are here," I used to joke. "Anybody could run this team."

Friends used to tell me, "Don't say those things. People might take them seriously."

Who cares? I didn't care if somebody took it seriously. It was my way of trying to make the game fun. It was also my way of trying to show people how good my coaching staff was. I believe people who do the job ought to get credit for it.

The Reds finished third in 1969. We went in there in 1970 and finished first with 102 wins. We won the division by fourteen games. I won't take away any credit from the players. They're the guys who played. They're the guys who won it. But what made them change from a third-place club into a winner? Did they drink some magic water over the winter?

All of a sudden people said this was an all-star team. All of a sudden the team could run on cruise control. Well, ain't that funny? They had basically the same guys in 1970 as they did the year before.

We added a couple of kids—Bernie Carbo and Hal McRae. Then we added Dave Concepcion. He was just a baby. Then we brought on Don Gullett. He was just nineteen and raw as a carrot. Over the next few years, we kept adding on. Ken Griffey. Dan Driessen. George Foster. Cesar Geronimo.

When those kids came up, they didn't know how to play in the major leagues. Griffey needed a lot of work in the outfield and George Scherger worked his tail off helping him to learn. Concepcion had the tools at shortstop but he needed a lot of polish, and Alex Grammas spent hour after hour teaching him the tricks.

Concepcion was really a key. He was a twenty-one-year-old kid out of Venezuela when he joined us. Imagine how he felt. Playing shortstop in the big leagues is tough enough, but David had to do it at twenty-one, in a foreign country, and on artificial turf for the first time in his life.

Alex Grammas came with me as a coach in 1970. He was a major league infielder for ten years and went right to work on David. Grammas and David sweat and bled from all the work they put in together.

Grammas hit David more ground balls than Donald Trump has dollar bills. Over and over again throughout batting practice every day, Concepcion fielded grounder after grounder.

And Grammas taught him to concentrate on situations. It wasn't good enough to field the ball. He had to learn what to do after he got it.

David was a great student. He was anxious to learn. He worked awfully hard and paid attention. He was so grateful for Grammas's hard work that he named his first son Alejandro.

Larry Shepard was my pitching coach and he worked harder than a one-armed lumberjack. We were never blessed with the greatest pitching staff so Larry had to work extra hard to make all the pieces fit together.

We had what I call a defensive pitching staff, not an offensive one. We had to work to keep it from exploding in our faces. I made a lot of pitchers unhappy because I was always taking pitchers out. Shepard did a great job of keeping them away from me, and of keeping it all together.

Yes, those kids had talent. I was blessed with some of the greatest players ever assembled on one team. But it was my coaching staff that spent so much time with them. They brought them along and helped to mold them into excellent players.

Nobody gave my coaching staff any credit. That's the thing that bothered me. People thought everything was just laying there for them.

The same thing happened when we went to Detroit. A lot of

the critics said, "Sparky had a push-button team in Cincinnati. He'll be lucky just to finish the season in Detroit."

We had good young talent when we came to Detroit. You could see all of the youngsters that were getting ready to bloom. They had the talent, but they didn't know how to win.

With everybody's help, we turned that around. We finished over .500 for ten straight years. In 1983 we won ninety-two games with a team that had no business finishing that high. In 1984 we came back with 104 wins and took the whole shooting match.

Yes, the players won those games. But it took the efforts of the entire organization.

Roger Craig was with me in Detroit. He has to be one of the finest pitching coaches in the history of the game. He's not only a good teacher; he also knows how to motivate his staff. He keeps them pumped up and ready to pitch. Everyone knows his role.

Alan Trammell and Lou Whitaker developed into the best shortstop—second-base combination around. They were still green when we got there. Grammas worked with both of them. So did Dick Tracewski, who's coached for the Tigers since 1973.

Never again in my career will I apologize for any success I might enjoy. Not anymore. I am tired of apologizing for winning at Cincinnati and Detroit "just because we had good players."

I'm grateful to those players. They all know how I feel about them. But I'm also grateful to my staff. They helped to show a lot of good young players what it takes to win.

I was prepared to sit out the entire 1979 season. I was getting paid for the last year of my contract with Cincinnati and I was working part-time for a TV station in Los Angeles. I wanted to get back to managing, but not until the 1980 season. Suddenly things changed.

The Tigers were playing in Anaheim the weekend of June 9. George Kell is one of the Tiger television broadcasters. He called to ask if I would be interested in appearing on his pregame show that Saturday. I told him I appreciated the offer, but I really didn't want to drive all the way to Anaheim from Thousand Oaks.

While we were talking, George said he'd heard through the grapevine that I was getting ready to make a decision about returning to managing. I told him he was right, but that I wasn't going to go back until 1980. I told him I was going to finalize that decision in about ten days.

At the time, I didn't know that George was feeling me out. I also didn't know how close he is to Jim Campbell who runs the Tigers.

Two days later, I got a call from Campbell. At first it was just idle talk. He asked me what I was looking for to return as a manager.

"You don't want to get involved with this," I told him.

He wanted to know. So I told him I wanted a five-year contract and exactly how much money was involved.

My wife told me I was crazy for asking what I did.

"No I'm not," I told her. "If I go back, it's on my terms. I'm not going to go through the same thing again."

I told every club that was interested in me the same thing. I told them exactly what I wanted. I didn't play one club against the other by upping the figures. I don't operate that way.

The figure I had in mind, at the time, sounded really high. But every club was willing to pay it. I have never negotiated a contract publicly and I won't start now. Except for Jim Campbell and me, no one ever will know exactly how much I got when I went to the Tigers or what I earn now. At the time I signed though, the contract made me the highest paid manager in the major leagues.

Campbell called back to see if I would be interested in the Tigers. In fact, he called several times. Finally on the sixth call, I agreed. I asked him not to say anything to anyone until I called the other six clubs that had shown interest. I didn't want them hearing that I was going to another club from anyone but me.

I was able to reach the right person at each of those clubs that same day.

On Tuesday, June 12, the Tigers announced I was their new manager. On Thursday, June 14, I managed my first game in a Tiger uniform.

I don't know exactly why the Detroit offer seemed so right. The Tigers met my conditions, but it wasn't just the money. I probably could have made more if I wanted to shop myself around.

I remembered the Tigers from spring training. I remembered all those fine young players. Alan Trammell and Lou Whitaker were just coming up. So were Jack Morris and Lance Parrish. And I remembered Kirk Gibson hitting a ball over the scoreboard that must have gone nine miles. He followed that with a routine ground ball he beat out for a hit.

"My God, this guy isn't human," I said to Alex Grammas. "This guy's got a chance to be great."

I think the real thing that convinced me was the Tiger organization. The Tigers are tradition. The Tigers are baseball history.

One of the best managers of our time was Ralph Houk. He once told me that if I ever had a chance to work for Jim Campbell and the Tigers to take it. He said I'd never be treated more professionally than by the Tigers. He couldn't have been more accurate.

My times in Cincinnati were special. I'll never forget those people. I'll never forget all those wonderful things that happened to me. But I can honestly say that my happiest years in baseball have been with the Tigers. I'll never get treated fairer by anybody than I have been treated by Jim Campbell and the Tigers.

In my case, being fired was the best thing that happened to me. It doesn't always work that way. But sometimes I don't think we give it a chance. We don't take the time to recognize the opportunities that are given to us.

Nobody likes to get beat up on. Nobody likes to fail. I'm

convinced, though, that you fail only if you think you've failed. If you think you're failing, then you have. If you know in your heart you're doing the best you can do, then you're not a failure. You have no control over what other people think of you. You only have control over how you think of yourself.

I don't know how long I'll manage in Detroit. Nobody does. When I leave Detroit, though, I doubt I'll ever go back to managing. I think when you reach a certain age and you've been in a place you love so much for so long, it's tough to move on.

Right now, I'm not about to worry about that. I'm happy. Like I told my son Albert almost twelve years ago, there are ways to turn defeat into victory.

Success

Success is for the moment . . . and only that moment.
I'm not smart enough to dream up something like that. But I am wise enough to appreciate what it means.

Vin Scully is the person who came up with the best definition of success that I've ever heard. We were in Los Angeles when I asked what success meant to him. As quickly as I asked him, that's how fast I got the answer.

"For the moment . . . and only that moment."

Vin Scully is a giant in the broadcasting world. From the World Series to the Masters, Vin has covered almost every major event. His field is sports, but I believe he could have been good in anything. He's well paid, he travels all around the world, he knows all kinds of influential people. Just last All-Star Game he shared the microphone with President Ronald Reagan.

To meet him, though, you'd swear he's just the guy next door. That's because he's a genuine person. He cares about his family. He cares about his friends. He cares about the people he works with. That's why when he defined *success*, there was no mention of money. There was no mention of power. His concern was performance.

The Dodgers held a function at Dodger Stadium in 1982 to celebrate Scully's winning the Ford Frick Award, which put him into the broadcaster's wing of Baseball's Hall of Fame. The place was packed. There were so many people who wanted to share Scully's happiness that it looked like a big New Year's celebration. There were a lot of players, former players, baseball executives, all kinds of members of the media, politicians, and a lot of little people that Scully has such a fondness for.

Peter O'Malley is the owner of the Dodgers. What he got up and said was a perfect reflection of Scully, who has broadcast Dodger games for as long as I can remember.

"I'm speaking for my father, myself, and everybody in the Dodger organization—past and present," O'Malley said.

"Vin Scully is the only man in the history of the Dodgers who never once has asked for a favor."

That may not sound like much. But think about it for a moment. Here's a man who could demand pretty much whatever he desires. Yet he doesn't place himself above anyone and has trouble asking anybody for something more than the time of day.

In 1982 Scully also had his star placed on Hollywood's Walk of Fame. That's pretty good for someone who started out merely by calling balls and strikes.

I've always been fascinated by success and what people think success is. I hate to say it, but I bet if you ask most people to define success, 99 percent somehow would link it to money.

Money is nice. But having a lot of money doesn't make someone a success. Most people who have big bank accounts are jerks. In fact, money and success are two totally different things. I try to explain this to every young player.

Baseball is one of the craziest lifestyles anyone could imagine. You couldn't dream up anything crazier. We're a bunch of grown men dressed in knickers. We fly first class all over the country. We stay in top-notch hotels. They give us more meal money than I can spend in a day. Everything we say is quoted in newspapers across the country. We appear on television all the time.

All we've got to do is play a simple game of baseball. And to do it, they pay us more money than I ever believed existed in this world. That's better than make-believe. It's like sticking up a bank with a water pistol and having the teller thank you as you walk out the door. It's a license to steal.

Baseball is a make-believe world. It ain't real. The guy carrying the lunchbox, taking the bus to work so that he can feed a houseful of kids—he's in the real world. The wife going to work after sending the kids to school—she's in the real world.

I like to recall the old story Lee Trevino told when he was asked about pressure on the PGA Tour. Someone said, "Lee, do you feel pressure when you're on the last hole of a tournament and you're putting for one hundred thousand dollars?"

Trevino shot back, "That isn't pressure. Pressure is when you're playing somebody for ten dollars and you've only got five dollars in your pocket. That's real pressure."

The guy out there trying to hustle ten bucks is real. All this other stuff is make-believe.

Because of all the money, publicity, and adulation from the fans, it's easy to get tricked once you become part of the game. It's easy to think how important we are. It's easy for fans to think that all ball players are successful, and if that's what they judge it on, they're 100 percent wrong. None of that stuff means a thing if the player ain't a real human being.

That's what I try to impress on all my young players. There's nothing wrong with trying to earn as much money as possible for yourself and for your family. The best performance deserves the most money. That's the way it should be. That's the way it is throughout our society. But I also try to make them see that all the money in the world doesn't guarantee success. To be successful, they must be good people or all the money in the world ain't worth the paper it's printed on.

Success doesn't carry a dollar sign. You can't buy it. You can't sell it—and it's only for the moment. If a man is a true success, he continually strives to be the best time after time after time.

One of the best examples is a good friend of mine. Bo Schembechler has been the head football coach at the University of Michigan for twenty years. His teams finish in the top ten every year. He's won Rose Bowls, Cotton Bowls, and more big games than most coaches ever get a chance to play. He's the best college coach in the country.

A few years ago, Bo had a fantastic offer to coach at Texas A&M. By the time he would have been done negotiating, he could have owned the Alamo.

He listened. Then he chose to stay at Michigan. Why? Because Bo has unquestionable loyalty to his university and the program he's developed. His commitment to all the kids he recruited and all the kids who sweat and bled for him over the years could not be sold for money. Bo refused to sell out.

I believe Bo Schembechler can wake up every morning and walk up to the mirror and say, "Hi, Mr. Schembechler. You are an outstanding person." He has that ability to love himself.

That's a tremendous gift. There's nothing wrong with that. If someone is a good person and is trying to do the right things in life, he should love himself. If you don't love yourself, how in the world can you expect anyone else to love you? If you think you are a jerk, then you're asking other people to love a jerk. That ain't right.

Money has never taken over Bo Schembechler's life. He has a goal and he's strong enough to stick to it. His goal is to be the most successful football coach in the country. Not just on the field, but also in preparing all the young men that fall under his influence. Bo makes sure once they leave their football helmets and pads at the university, they are prepared to tackle the game of life.

Bo is committed to fulfill every promise he made to those young men's parents when he recruited those kids. I guarantee you that in his twenty years, he's upheld every promise he made and did his level best to prepare those young men to deal with life. He does not have to look backward or sideways or down at the floor. That is true success.

I always return to Detroit during the winter just before I go to spring training. We have a lot of media functions and parties to help let people know that baseball is right around the corner.

We had a free evening one Saturday a few years ago and I went to dinner with a few friends, including Schembechler. The owner of the restaurant sat us in the corner and I had my back to the dining room. Bo was sitting across from me and had a clear view of the whole room.

I noticed that he kept looking at one particular table across the room. There was a young boy in a wheelchair who couldn't keep his eyes off Bo. I knew that boy wanted to come over and get Bo's autograph or at least shake his hand. I could tell he was shy, though, and wouldn't think of actually doing it.

When dinner was over, Bo got up without saying a word. While we went to get our coats, Bo walked over to that other table and put his hands on that young boy's shoulders.

"You know, I've been watching you all night and I felt that I just wanted to say hello and shake your hand," Bo said. "You look like a fine young man."

Of course, the boy was flabbergasted. The look in his parents' eyes was priceless.

Bo signed an autograph and quietly left. Just a tiny act with a gigantic meaning.

Dean Smith at the University of North Carolina is another. I bet Dean Smith has had several opportunities to coach in the NBA. But he chose to stick with his program because he's committed to those kids. He showed me real guts in the 1989 NCAA Tournament when, for disciplinary purposes, he didn't allow his star player to start a game that easily could have been lost.

John Wooden won all those NCAA basketball titles at UCLA. There was never a hint of a scandal in all those years. He built men. Then he left. He never changed along the way. He set the example and then lived by it. That's success.

Give me $10 million right now. Come back and see me in three years and I guarantee you I'll have $30 million. I've never been to college, but it doesn't take a genius to figure that out. Does that make me successful? No. It only proves the old saying that it takes money to make money. It has nothing to do with success.

Success is the person who year after year after year reaches the highest limits in his field. It doesn't matter what that field is—ball player, banker, truck driver, painter, lawyer, doctor, mailman.

But on top of all that, he must be a good person.

I feel no compassion for the person who strikes it rich and then doesn't know how to act with his fortune. His good luck turns into the worst luck he could have.

People say the money changed him. It's not his fault he turned out like that.

Baloney! The money had nothing to do with it. He didn't change a bit. He was a jerk before he made the money and now he's a jerk with it. His problem now is that everybody knows it.

He was fortunate to make money. But he was never successful. He thinks he's important. But he ain't worth a dime. He can't be called a success.

The most successful people I know carry a lunchbox to work. My daddy did. He raised a houseful of kids and never bought a thing for himself. But he paid all the bills and gave us more love than any other kids had. There isn't a man more successful than the one whose income must be budgeted so closely so that he can raise beautiful kids.

The successful person is the man who knows how to deal

with every person in every walk of life. It doesn't matter if it's the president of a bank or the guy who just had his bank account canceled. The successful person treats those two the same. The successful person makes everyone feel important. Whenever you're around him, you feel at peace. He makes everybody feel at ease because he never changes. You don't see him up one day, then down the next. He's not happy just when things are going good. People around him never know when the successful man is having a problem.

The successful person makes every day feel like a birthday. There's cake and ice cream for everybody. He's content with himself and he makes people happy. He's successful and he knows it. Now he must share that good feeling.

How does a person attain success?

Longevity. Because success is for the moment . . . and only that moment. So it must be acquired moment after moment after moment. That's the difference and that's where a lot of people make a mistake. In baseball, for instance, some guys think if they win one year that they're automatically successful.

They're wrong. That's not success. All that happened was the blind squirrel happened to find an acorn. They could never repeat because they don't have it in them. They were for the moment. But only for one single moment.

When I first came to Detroit in 1979 I looked through all the Tiger records. Hughie Jennings managed the Tigers for fourteen seasons and holds the club record with 1,131 wins.

I remember saying, "My God, how can I ever catch that man?"

Now I know I've got a chance. I believe I'll even pass him.

I won't say that makes me successful. I'll let others make that judgment. But I know what I expect of myself. Wins and losses on the field affect the team. But they'll never change the standards by which I live.

The successful person is not a one-time Charlie. He doesn't hit-and-miss and just hope that next year is better. Win or lose, he sticks by his standards. He doesn't pop off when things fall his way and he doesn't cry when his troops are falling around him.

He's there to lean on when the going gets tough. He doesn't break his own rules to make things easy for himself. Everybody knows exactly where he stands. He lets everybody know they're not fighting the battle alone.

Success is accompanied by awesome responsibility. Heroes are hard to find. They must take the lead. The successful person can't go halfway to meet the other person in the middle. He's got to take the extra step to show that other person he really cares.

In spring training a while back, we played the Red Sox in Winter Haven. In batting practice before the game, a man walked up to shake my hand.

"Hi Sparky, I'm Ted Williams," he said.

I almost fell over. I started to laugh.

"Ted, that's the funniest thing I ever heard," I said.

"What do you mean?" he said.

"You telling me that you're Ted Williams," I answered. "Everybody knows you. You don't have to say who you are."

"No, Sparky, it can't be that way," he explained. "I would never want you to be embarrassed if you happened to forget who I was."

Now just imagine. This was Ted Williams. This was one of the greatest players in the history of our game making sure that I wasn't embarrassed.

That's not only success. That's class.

After that, I never meet anyone to whom I don't introduce myself before the other guy gets a chance. I always walk up with my hand out. "Hi, Sparky Anderson."

It's not much. Just a little touch. But it makes the other person feel important. And what's so bad about making another person feel good?

We've got a Hall of Famer in Detroit named Al Kaline. I honestly believe if Kaline wanted to run for governor of Michigan, he'd win. But he's not that type. In fact, he's exactly the opposite.

I've been to many functions with Kaline where he's gone

around introducing himself to people, almost apologizing that he didn't know their names. He never asks for anything special. In fact, it's hard for him to understand why so many people want to do things for him.

Sandy Koufax is the same way. He's another Hall of Famer who was one of the greatest pitchers of all time.

I used to host a golf tournament during the off-season in Thousand Oaks to raise money for the local college. A lot of major league players, former players, and show business entertainers used to participate. I put one celebrity in each foursome. The businessmen who paid a good price to participate were wild over being able to play with an honest-to-goodness celebrity.

I asked Sandy if he would honor us by playing in my tournament. He said, of course, he would do it. But then I had to convince him that he was playing free. That's how down-to-earth he is, and that's how nicely he treats all the people around him.

There's a poster I keep over my desk at Tiger Stadium. It's called "A Short Course in Human Relations," and it reads:

> The Six Most Important Words:
>   I admit I made a mistake.
> The Five Most Important Words:
>   You Did a Good Job.
> The Four Most Important Words:
>   What Is Your Opinion?
> The Three Most Important Words:
>   If You Please.
> The Two Most Important Words:
>   Thank You.
> The One Most Important Word:
>   We.
> The Least Important Word:
>   I.

There isn't a successful person in the world that doesn't share this philosophy.

The truly successful person is the one who protects everybody around him. The people in front. The people in back. The people to the right. And the people to the left.

He deals fairly and honestly with everyone around him. The people he works with every day. And the people he might see only on occasion. He ropes everyone into his system and he pulls the cord. But he never lets them know because he would never embarrass anyone.

The successful person never raises his voice. He doesn't have to. People listen.

He's not afraid to give credit where it's due. He's wise enough to know it will all be paid back.

Success isn't something that just happens. A person doesn't just wake up one day and suddenly become successful. Success is learned. Success is practiced. And then it's shared with everyone around him.

Success is for the moment . . . and only that moment.

June 5, 1989: The day I returned to the Tigers.

I demonstrate the style that earned me the nickname "Sparky."

I let the umps know what I think, as Johnny Bench—the best player at his position in the history of baseball—looks on.

As a player when Toronto was a minor league team.

Taking a swing during my one year as a major league player—with Philadelphia in 1959.

With then-Tigers manager Ralph Houk before a sandlot benefit game in
Cincinnati.

Tommy Lasorda and I have a lot in common: We both love to talk.

I consider Oakland manager Tony La Russa one of the brightest young minds in the game.

Alex Grammas is one of the coaches I've leaned on throughout my career.

With Tigers president Jim Campbell (left) and American League president Dr. Bobby Brown.

Jack Morris douses me with champagne after the Tigers won the 1984 World Series. Jim Campbell, Kirk Gibson, and Bill Lajoie stand to my left.

I have a tremendous amount of respect for Hall of Famer Al Kaline.

Pete Rose is the toughest competitor who ever lived.

I don't claim to have the looks of Jim Palmer, but I enjoy discussing baseball with him.

President Gerald Ford discovers I love to talk.

With Governor James J. Blanchard of Michigan.

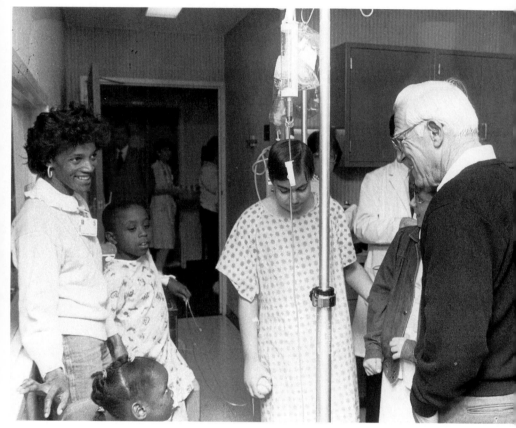

I enjoy my weekly visits to Children's and Henry Ford hospitals.

With my wife and best friend, Carol.

— *I love TV . . .*

. . . and I love the fans.

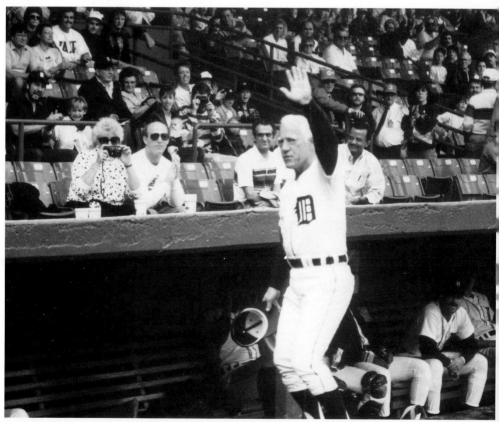

Players, Past
and Present

P eople who live in the past generally are afraid to compete in
the present.

I didn't read that in a fortune cookie. I just know it's true.
People get stuck thinking about how good it was "back then."
They're so hooked on the past that the present slips right by.
Forget about the future—they don't even appreciate what's going
on now.

I've got my faults, but living in the past isn't one of them.
There's no future in it. It just can't be done. I'm a right-now
person. This is where I'm living. This is what I have to do. I can't
worry about the way things used to be. I can't wonder if things
were better a long time ago.

What good does that do? It only takes away the energy I have to tackle the problems that face me right now. Let's deal with the right now. What was, was. What is, is. What will be ... who knows? So why worry about it?

I've been very lucky. My teams have won three World Series. I've got a championship ring for each one of them. I'm proud of them, but I never wear any of them. My oldest son, Lee, has my World Series ring from 1975. My second son, Albert, has the one from 1976. My 1984 ring is in a safe-deposit box. It belongs to my grandson, George.

Don't get me wrong. Each one of those rings means a lot to me. That's why I gave them to my sons and grandson. I don't mean disrespect for those people who wear a World Series ring. They earned it. They should be proud. I just don't like to go around with a big diamond ring on my finger showing everybody that I won a World Series. I know where I've been. I know what I've done. Let's get on with trying to win another one right now. Not next year or the year after that. Right now.

There are a lot of people in baseball who have trouble working their way out of the past.

"These guys can't play baseball the way we used to play," they say. "So and so here couldn't have made our bench."

They're only fooling themselves. Do they really believe the players back then were better than the ones we have today?

If they do, they're watching a different game than I am.

I mean no disrespect for the giants who helped make baseball what it is today. They were great in their time. They worked hard. They played hard. They earned every penny they got and all the glory that went with it.

I don't blame some of the old-timers for holding onto their memories. But let's be honest. There's really no comparison. Players today are much better athletes than the players from the past.

The way things change so quickly now, players twenty years from now will be even better. Players will get stronger. They'll run and throw a little faster. The game will get better all the way around.

Strictly for baseball fundamentals, I believe the game peaked in the 1950s. That was primarily because of the genius of Branch Rickey. He was a baseball scientist. What Abner Doubleday invented, Mr. Rickey perfected. He was the greatest innovator this game has ever known. He had the sharpest mind baseball ever saw.

The people who worked for and learned from Rickey went on to become giants themselves. People like Walter Alston, Gene Mauch, Leo Durocher, Herman Franks, Don Zimmer, Dick Williams, Tommy Lasorda, Roger Craig . . . the list goes on and on.

If ever there was a Golden Age for fundamentals, it had to be in the 1950s. That's when Rickey's influence was at its peak. That's when the game was played sharper and with more intensity than at any other period.

There are other reasons, too. The war was over. Minor leagues flourished. There was an abundance of talent with ten fewer major league teams than today. And baseball drew the cream of the crop.

Professional football never really got to be what it is today until television turned it into a billion-dollar industry. The same is true for basketball. The NBA now brags about having the finest athletes in the world. But twenty years ago, the NBA was still a baby.

The NHL had only six teams. And all of those players came from Canada.

Golf and tennis belonged to the rich people. A kid growing up never went to the golf course or tennis court unless his daddy was a member of some fancy country club. Those sports didn't belong to all the people.

Everybody played baseball. It didn't matter if you were rich or poor. It didn't matter if you were big or small. It didn't matter if you were black or white. Everybody played ball.

Some organizations like the Dodgers and Cardinals had

twenty or thirty teams in their systems. Imagine how much competition there was just to step up one rung of the ladder every spring. A player better learn the fundamentals if he didn't want to spend his career in Podunk eating hot dogs and chasing ground balls on some rock-hard infield.

Baseball was the game to play. Every outstanding athlete from every school across the country dreamed about growing up to be a big league ball player. It didn't matter if he was a great quarterback or a great shooting guard. That young man dreamed about hitting home runs in the big leagues.

The competition was fierce. Baseball had a lock on the market.

Today all sports have exploded into big business. There are millions and millions of dollars in every sport. Now the choice between baseball and football takes a little more thought. The high school hotshot might choose to play football in front of 75,000 people at a big-time university instead of spending a few years on some dusty minor league field.

The same holds true for the basketball standout. Playing in the NCAA Tournament is a lot more appealing than long bus rides through minor league towns.

Money in all sports has shot through the roof. It's like playing with Monopoly money and there is no limit. A young man knows if he can make it big at a four-year college, he's got a chance to cash in for life.

The competition doesn't stop at college or with the NFL and NBA. There are twenty-one teams in the NHL. Most of the players still come from Canada. But now there are more Americans than ever before. That number will continue to grow and take away more athletes from baseball.

Golf and tennis no longer belong only to the rich. They're still not as popular as the team sports, but more and more they're attracting the athlete who can excel in whatever sport he chooses.

So competition for the premier athlete has become fierce among the sports. That competition, however, has produced a modern athlete that is physically far superior to most who played in the past.

Size, conditioning, and money are the three most significant factors to revolutionize the change in today's athlete.

When I was a young player in the Dodger system, I blended in with most of the guys in camp. I was five foot nine, about 160 pounds. That's small, but I didn't look out of place. In fact, that was the problem. So many of us looked so much alike. I was always worried that they'd mistake me for someone else. I always hoped it was for somebody that was up for promotion to a higher league.

Back then if we had a player that was six foot three, he was somewhat of a freak. If he was a hitter, he was a gorilla. He could smack the ball four hundred feet. If he was a pitcher, he could throw the ball through a brick wall. Nobody wanted to face him in batting practice. Nobody wanted to be embarrassed.

Look at most of the pitching staffs now. Almost every nine-man staff averages out at six foot three or even six foot four.

Today the small kid is the freak. He might still make it, but it's easier for him to get lost in the shuffle. The guys today are monsters.

This applies to all sports. In baseball, the ball flies faster. In football, the players are walking condominiums. In basketball, the players play above the rim. Even professional bowlers seem bigger today.

Remember the Four Horsemen at Notre Dame? They were good. But do you honestly think they could have competed against the likes of Bo Jackson, Herschel Walker, Walter Payton, or Tony Dorsett? Of course, they couldn't! Today we can't even imagine a major college where the top cat in the backfield weighs 150 pounds. At the major schools today, they bring in running backs from high school that already weigh 210 to 220 pounds.

It's the same thing in basketball. In his day, there was nobody better than George Mikan. Nobody touched him. He was king of the court. Was George Mikan ever as good as Kareem Abdul-Jabbar? What about Magic Johnson, Michael Jordan, or Dominique Wilkens? Absolutely not. George Mikan today would have a tough time making a major college team. That's plain fact. Stars back then were stars of their times. Those times are long gone.

Today's athlete generally looks like a Greek god who just stepped out of some body-building ad. These guys could kick sand in Charles Atlas's face. I notice it a little more every year in spring training.

When I first started managing I never knew what condition players would show up in. I might be counting on my number one pitcher to check in fifteen pounds lighter than where he finished last season. When he showed up twenty-five heavier, I knew I had a problem—forty pounds worth.

The reason that happened is simple. Back then, most of the players still weren't making the big bucks. Most had to work during the off-season. When February came around, they quit their jobs and headed for spring training.

They weren't able to work out every day during the winter like today's players. Nowadays the boys don't have to work. They make enough money to wait until next spring. Most belong to health spas. They show up for spring training in midseason shape.

They eat differently today. Most guys watch their diets. A lot of them are into health foods.

Players still drink beer. But not like they used to. In the old days, that was almost a status symbol. A player wasn't macho unless he hung out with the boys guzzling some beer. You don't see that as much anymore.

Players don't smoke cigarettes like they used to. In the old days, walking into the clubhouse was like walking into a fog. It was macho to have a cigarette in your hand.

All these things have changed the players. They're stronger. They're much better conditioned. Just think what it would be like to field a team of old-timers in their prime and put them up against some of today's stars.

It would be murder—first degree murder. Today's players would absolutely destroy them.

Look at the size and physique of today's players. I've seen pictures of the old-timers. I've seen them on old newsreels. They were mostly little short guys. None of them stepped out of an ad for a health spa. I never saw a Jose Canseco.

I love watching those old film clips. I saw a movie from 1927. Some say that's when the Yankees had the best team that ever was. The catcher had a tiny screen for a mask and a little dinky glove. He wore little shin guards and was standing up to catch.

Just imagine! This was supposed to be the golden era of baseball. That's when the Yankees were the cock of the walk. The equipment they used can't compare to today's. How in the world could you compete in today's fast game with a little dinky glove that just fit your hand? How could you stop a ball in the hole after some six-foot-five gorilla hit it like a rocket? It would be impossible.

They used to call Walter Johnson "The Big Train" because he threw so fast. There ain't a day gone by that Walter Johnson could ever throw the ball as fast as Nolan Ryan. Yes, Walter Johnson was a freight train at the time. But now the trains zip by a whole lot faster.

Ty Cobb is considered the king of base stealers. He stole ninety-six one year. They say he was so fast he could flip the switch, jump into bed, and get under the covers before the light went out.

Ty Cobb couldn't run with half of the guys playing today. That is not a slap at Ty Cobb. That's merely a tribute to today's modern athlete.

Of course, the great ones of today could have played in the old days, and the great ones of the old days could have played today's modern game because they, too, would have the benefit of all our advancements.

Paul Molitor would have been a superstar back in the twenties. He plays that scrappy, hustling style of baseball that would have clicked on any team.

Shoeless Joe Jackson probably would battle for the batting title if he were playing today. He was that good of a hitter and I'm sure he would have been that much better if he played today.

Don Mattingly and Lou Gehrig are tremendously similar. If you could switch them in time, there'd be no difference.

The same is true for Jose Canseco and Babe Ruth. Canseco doesn't have the charisma The Babe had. And The Babe never had the body Canseco has. But if you could flip-flop them in history, they'd both be successful.

Kirk Gibson reminds me of players from the old days. He plays that reckless, free-lance style that's a throwback to what a lot of people call "the good old days."

Ty Cobb, Rogers Hornsby, Honus Wagner, and players like that would have made it today, but they're just not the equals of today's superstars.

Players now are different to deal with, too. The basic difference is education. In the old days players came from the farms. They were coal miners, steelworkers, laborers from the fields. They got no money. They had to scuffle. They fought all the way. Man, they were mean. They chewed tobacco. They spit on people. But that was a way of life. They were tough, tough guys that refused to be hurt.

Today we're dealing with men who are better educated. They don't all have college degrees. But they've all been to school and have an idea of what the world is about.

Today's players won't do some of the things that the old-timers pulled. They're not out to hurt anybody. They're not going to spit or gouge or kick just to win a game. Today's player is out to win by beating his opponent according to the rules. It's talent against talent, but all within the rules.

That's the way it should be. An educated man is much easier to understand and teach. If he has education, he's trained to learn a lesson.

Compared to when I started, it's much easier for me to manage today. Now you can talk common sense to players. They know if they play their cards right, they can make enough money to set themselves up for life.

We don't have to dangle a carrot in front of them. They already know what's out there. The average salary is a half million a year. If a guy talks right, dresses sharp, and keeps his nose clean, he can pick up another pile doing the right things off the field.

When I first started playing, there was no money in the game. Even the so-called superstars had to work during the off-season. My first year playing I made $250 a month. That was for five months or $1,250 for the entire year. Things were cheaper then but there's no way a young family could live on that.

During the winter I had to hustle. I had more off-season jobs than an employment agency had entries. I was a painter. I worked as a laborer. I ran errands. One year I tried selling used cars. It was beautiful. I had to be the only used-car salesman in the whole state of California who spent more time telling young couples why they shouldn't buy a certain car they liked than trying to convince them it was made for them.

I couldn't help it. I knew what some of those cars were really like. There was no way I was going to let somebody spend their hard-earned dollars on them.

I used to scuffle so much that I almost quit baseball to look for a real job. As usual though, Carol was the wise one. She told me how miserable I'd be if I left the game without giving it the best shot I had. If it hadn't been for her, I would have been out of baseball before I even managed in the minor leagues. So I know what it was like to scuffle as a youngster.

Today it's totally different. The players don't have to scuffle during the off-season. They're all well paid. They all have fine homes. They all drive fancy cars. Walking through our parking lot is like walking through a showroom.

All this makes a difference with the game out on the field. Players know how much money is out there. They're going for the vault.

A lot of people argue that big money has stifled the game. They say that once a player gets it, there's nothing left to strive for.

That's a bunch of baloney. Why shouldn't a player want to make as much money as is up for grabs? He's no different than the people who go watch him play. Aren't they trying to make the most they can?

The old story about Rockefeller still holds true today. When asked how much is enough, he smiled and said, "Just a little bit more."

There's nothing wrong with that. That's the way it should be.

I think it's fantastic for a man to want to be the highest paid player in the history of the game. Because to reach that, he's got to put numbers on the board. Big numbers. To get those numbers, he's got to bust his butt. Nobody's going to give him the cash just because he's a nice guy. He's got to produce. He doesn't need any pushing. He'll push himself.

That's why I love getting players who were raised in the ghetto. There's something special about them. You can see it in their eyes. These cats fight and scrap all the way. They've had to do it all their lives on the street just to survive. A lot of them didn't live day-to-day; they lived hour-to-hour. Now they have the chance to make the big buck and they can make it for themselves and make it for their families.

These are the guys you want on your side when the going gets tough. You'll never know if you are successful unless you are poor first. It's impossible to know what success really means without that.

If you can make it, there isn't a greater feeling in the world. To watch a kid escape the ghetto and fight his way to the top is a tremendous feeling. Now he can walk tall.

They say any boy can grow up to become president of the United States if he really wants it. I don't believe that.

I do believe any boy can grow up to become a professional athlete if he's hungry enough. And when he does, he's a beautiful sight.

So have players changed? Of course they have.

Is managing different because of that change? No question about it.

Is baseball better because of it? Absolutely.

Baseball has always been blessed with tremendous players. Memories of these players give the game its color and charm.

I would never say anything to tarnish the accomplishments of those great players. I would never show disrespect. That would be a sin.

In his time, nobody threw the ball faster than Walter Johnson. In his time, nobody was faster than Ty Cobb. In his time, nobody hit the ball further than Babe Ruth.

But the key words are *in his time*.

Like everything else in our society, baseball has gone through all kinds of changes. There'll be more. That's good. That's the way it should be.

There used to be some great players. But today's batch are even better. And twenty years from now, they'll be even better.

I hope I'm around to see it. I hope I am never afraid of change. I hope I'm always right here and *now*.

Impact Players
and Clutch Players

One of the newer terms in baseball is the "impact player." This is the guy who might not have all the fancy statistics but when he steps to the plate, people give up their spot in the hot dog line. Nobody wants to miss him. He's the guy who people stop for, look at, and listen to.

There's a difference between an impact player and a "clutch performer." The clutch performer is the guy who delivers when the game is on the line. When you need a big hit late in the game, somehow he comes up with one. If he's a pitcher, he gets the strikeout when nothing but a strikeout will do.

A lot of clutch performers go about their business so quietly and with such precision they almost go unnoticed. They get taken for granted.

The impact player can't help but be noticed. Normally he is a clutch performer. But even when he fails, he gets the crowd excited. What he may lack in statistics he makes up for in fan appeal. He's got charisma . . . pizzazz. He's explosive. He's got that unexplainable dramatic flair. Fans pay money to see him whether he smacks a homer or strikes out. He's a legitimate meal ticket.

Player agents love the term "impact player." They use it as a bargaining tool. If a client's statistics aren't so hot one year, the agent tries to make him into an impact player.

Nice try. But they're not fooling anybody. There ain't a fraction of the impact players agents would lead you to believe.

In my time, there are three guys who stand way above everybody else when it comes to impact. No one's bigger than the game itself. But these three guys are bigger than the rest who are playing it. They're Reggie Jackson, Pete Rose, and Dave Winfield. People paid money just to see them perform.

The tops for overall impact was Reggie Jackson—hands down. To me, Reggie Jackson was the Muhammad Ali of baseball.

A lot of people complain that Reggie ran off his mouth. They say he was more interested in promoting Reggie Jackson than he was trying to win a pennant.

They don't know what they're talking about. Like Reggie once said, "If you done it, it ain't bragging."

Reggie done it all. He did everything he talked about. He backed up every promise he ever made. And he did it with a certain style that baseball had never seen before.

Reggie Jackson probably won more big games than any other player in history. He not only won them, he told you he'd win them. In the process he sold a lot of tickets.

He did it over an entire career. It wasn't just for one, two, or three years. The man started talking early and kept producing until it was late. Every club he played for turned into a winner. That wasn't coincidence.

Reggie played for Oakland when the Athletics strung together one of the greatest teams in history for a five-year period. He played for the Yankees when they won their division four out of five years. Then he moved on to California and the Angels took two titles.

The man played in the big leagues for twenty years. In all of those years, his team won at least the division championship. He played in six World Series and his team won five times.

That ain't coincidence. That's Reggie Jackson.

Baseball isn't a one-man show. To win any kind of championship, everyone must contribute. But I do not think those teams could have won without Reggie Jackson. He did more dynamic things in tight situations in key games than any player I can remember.

Reggie could hit for power. He could hit for average. He could steal a base. He could throw. He was an outstanding defensive outfielder early in his career. And Reggie took it one step further. He added an extra dimension. He did everything with his own special style. He was a tremendous showman. He was always on stage and he loved every minute.

Reggie had that special way of talking. He knew when to use *I*'s instead of *we*'s. He was the first player to talk about himself in the third person. Reggie said things like, "Reggie Jackson is going to have a big series."

Some writers thought Reggie was a put-on. But he was only telling the truth. How many guys would come right out and talk about themselves?

Reggie did. It sounded like simple bragging. But he did it in a humorous way. Then he backed up every single word.

Reggie lived the life every young boy dreams about. He made great catches to put his teams into the World Series. He crunched home runs to help his teams win the Series. He won MVPs. He hit 563 home runs. He got to be so popular he appeared in movies and on TV shows. Reggie did all this. And he called his shots all the way.

It's got to be a real rush to tell the world you're going to do something that's darn near impossible and then make good on the promise like it was all by design. There ain't a man alive who wouldn't love to do that. To tell the truth, there aren't too many guys around who wouldn't love to be Reggie Jackson.

Reggie did run his mouth. But he ran it in a good way. He backed everything he said and made baseball fun along the way. In my time, I don't think there was any player who did more for the game than Reggie Jackson.

We were playing in Anaheim a couple of years ago and I stopped Reggie during batting practice.

"I just want to tell you one thing," I told him. "A lot of people talk about all the great things you accomplished in baseball. I respect you for something else. The thing that makes you so great is that I never saw you not run out a ground ball as hard as you could."

That's a tremendous tribute. That shows he never cheated the fans. He never shortchanged his teammates.

"Thank you," he said. "That's one of the things I'm most proud of."

Reggie Jackson should be proud. He's a lock-cinch first-ballot Hall of Famer. Any writer who doesn't vote for him on the first ballot should have his privilege taken away for the rest of his life.

The same is true for Rose and Winfield. They are also first-ballot Hall of Famers. They played hard. They don't know any other way. Not once throughout their whole careers did you ever see Jackson, Rose, or Winfield not hustle.

Peter Edward Rose was unbelievable when it came to fan appeal. Peter Edward wanted to run up the records. He was obsessed by it and could tell you right where he stood every single day. But he played for the fans. That's why he played so hard.

When I was at Cincinnati, we played an exhibition game with our AAA club at Indianapolis. I planned to let my regular lineup bat once so the fans could see The Big Red Machine before I took them out. Peter Edward made an out the first time up. When I started to make the switch, he asked if he could bat one more time. I said okay but that he was coming out after he hit. I didn't want him getting hurt in an exhibition game.

Next time up, Peter Edward lined a single over second base. I had no idea why he wanted to bat again until I saw him rounding first. Then it dawned on me. Peter Edward never slowed down after he rounded first. Halfway between first and second, he took off like a runaway freight train with the engine steaming. When he got near second, there it came—his famous belly slide. The crowd started to cheer as if Elvis had just walked into the park. Peter Edward was safe. He stood up, dusted himself off and signaled me to send in a pinch runner.

As he trotted in, the crowd was standing. It was going wild. When he got in the dugout he pulled me over and said, "That's what they came to see. Now they got their money's worth."

Peter Edward knew what the fans wanted. He never let them down.

Winfield has such tremendous presence that he naturally commands attention. Winfield is so tall, so powerful, that it looks like he takes three steps and he's already on first base. In the outfield, he covers so much ground it looks like he plays two positions. When he stands in the batter's box and extends his arms, it looks like he can touch the pitcher. That pitcher can feel Winfield breathing right down his neck.

Nobody connects on a ball like Winfield. Once I saw him hit a line drive that just cleared our shortstop's head. It kept right on sailing and carried all the way over the left field fence. A couple inches lower and our shortstop could have caught it. But he hit it so hard it took off like a low flying rocket.

He always seems to do something dramatic. Big hit or big catch, he wins games.

I'll never forget a game in Detroit in 1983 when he simply overpowered a pitch over the right field fence for a three-run game-winning homer in the ninth.

Detroit fans know baseball. You can't fool them. So when Winfield came up with the Yankees trailing by two, they could sense the drama. I sure felt it in the dugout, and I didn't like it one bit.

We got two quick strikes on Winfield. Just for a second, I thought we could get out of it for a change. He got jammed on his hands with the next pitch and still was strong enough to push the ball over the right field fence.

Playing in New York in those white pinstripes gives him even more magic. The fact that he could withstand all that pressure with the Yankees and handle himself with grace proved he's a big person inside as well as outside.

Reggie, Rose, and Winfield are in a class by themselves when it comes to impact. Yet I was lucky at Cincinnati to have four players who could break up a game when the chips were down. Peter Edward Rose, Johnny Bench, Joe Morgan, and Tony Perez.

Rose had tremendous appeal to the fans, but Bench was just behind him. Both were deadly in clutch situations.

Bench was the greatest catcher that ever lived. No one ever played his position better than he did. He also delivered key hits all the time.

John hit the greatest single home run for me that I ever saw in my twenty years of managing. It was 1972 in the playoffs against Pittsburgh. It was Game Five and we went into the last of the ninth trailing 3–2. The Pirates brought in Dave Giusti to face Bench leading off. John drilled one over the right field fence to tie the score. As soon as he hit that I knew we had it won. We got two singles and a fly ball before Bob Moose uncorked a wild pitch allowing George Foster to score. But the hit that won it was John's home run.

It was just one home run. But it was how he hit it and when he hit it. That's the way he was throughout his career. In All-Star Games he hit home runs. In the playoffs he hit home runs. In the World Series he hit home runs. He always rose to the occasion.

He was big with the fans even when he didn't do anything. I

remember one night in Philadelphia walking to the bus after the game. When John walked out of the ballpark, people swarmed him as if he were some kind of rock star. He had just struck out four times. But it didn't matter to them. John had such tremendous presence, it was well deserved.

With the game on the line, Tony Perez was probably the most dynamic player I ever saw. If he had a chance to beat you in the eighth or ninth, he had you beat. He was more reliable than the monthly mortgage bill. He had tremendous impact on the field, but he didn't have that special link with the fans. They loved him, but it was never like it was for Rose and Bench.

The other great one was my second baseman. For a four-year span, Joe Morgan was the greatest single player I ever saw in my lifetime. And I will never live long enough to see a man have four consecutive years like he had. The man averaged more than .300. He averaged 20 home runs, 30 doubles, and 90 RBIs. He stole 50 to 60 bases. He even walked an average of 120 times.

The way he stole bases I figure he averaged more than a hundred doubles a year. He'd get on base, then steal another one. That's like having a hundred doubles. And he was so smart. He was like a manager on the field. He knew the game like no other player did. He should be managing today. For a four-year stretch, you ain't never going to find another player to match Joe Morgan.

Bench deservedly won the MVP one year. Rose deservedly won it another. Morgan won it twice and could have won it all four. If he had, nobody could have said a word. That's how great a player he was. Until Joe did it four years in a row, I don't think fans across the country really knew how to appreciate him.

But again, Rose and Bench cast such a giant shadow when it came to the fans, sometimes Joe got overlooked.

After Joe's first year with us, I had his locker moved next to Rose. One day Joe walked into my office.

"You're pretty sharp," he said. "I figured out why you moved me next to Rose. You like the way he plays. I guess you must like my style, too."

"Oh . . . I wouldn't do that," I told him.

But he knew. I wanted to cram as much charisma as possible into one corner of the room so all the other players could look over there and see what hustle is all about.

Rose, Bench, Perez, and Morgan. How lucky can one man be? All were clutch players.

Morgan was the steadiest. He ran at an even keel. There weren't a lot of low points. He ran basically on high.

Rose was pretty much the same. To get two hundred hits a year, he had to stay steady. Once in a while though, he'd taper off. Then he'd get in a groove to make up for lost ground.

Bench and Perez were a lot alike. When they got hot, it was awesome. They'd drill anything the pitcher threw up there. They'd hit it hard and long.

All four have to go into the Hall of Fame. It wouldn't be fair if one or two or three made it and the other guy didn't.

I've seen other clutch hitters who really get going when the game's on the line. It seems like they just sit back till it's do-or-die time. Then they jump up to strike like a rattler.

In all my years in baseball, the one man I absolutely hated to face with the game on the line was Willie McCovey. To me, he was the most awesome creature ever to walk into the batter's box. If the ball was in the strike zone, I knew it was going to get hit hard someplace.

Funny thing is, though, Willie never hurt me that much. That's because I walked McCovey probably three times as often as other managers did. I simply refused to be hurt by him. I had so much respect for that man there was no sense in testing him. I knew he could hurt me. He knew he could hurt me. So what was the sense in proving it?

Willie Stargell was a lot like McCovey. But I gambled a little more with Stargell than I did with McCovey. Stargell was a launcher. Once in a while he'd chase some bad pitches. McCovey had that great eye. He made you come to him.

McCovey had that laid-back style about him. He was like that big, old, gentle giant who wasn't going to bother anybody. No . . . he wasn't going to bother anyone. Not until the time came. Then he was going to bother you real bad.

He was an awesome power hitter. I honestly think he flattened some balls. I wish McCovey could have spent his career in one of these smaller parks. Detroit would have been a great park for him. If McCovey had played in Detroit and there was a rule that you couldn't walk him, I guarantee you he would have hit eighty home runs a year. If you weren't allowed to walk him and he got his six hundred at bats, eighty homers would have been a lock. He would have hit thirty by accident and the other fifty would have been rocket launches.

The guy who did hurt me a lot was Steve Garvey. With the game on the line, Garvey could beat you with a base hit every time. If there was a man in scoring position with Garvey up late in the game, it was over. He found a way to get a hit. In my time in the National League, he was one of the best clutch hitters I faced.

The one hit by Garvey I remember better than any other came late in 1974 when we were making a run at the Dodgers. We pulled to within two games of them before Garvey's hit broke our backs.

We were in Los Angeles leading by two runs in the last of the eighth. The Dodgers loaded the bases with two out and I brought in Pedro Borbon to face Garvey. Borbon made some nasty pitches, but Garvey fouled off what he had to and then delivered a three-run double. That sealed the game and the season.

You had to get Garvey out before he got two strikes on him. With two strikes he became a defensive hitter and was almost always able to make a ball fall safely somewhere.

Ted Simmons was another one. I don't think there were ever very many catchers who could hit like Ted Simmons. He wasn't like Bench. John was death and destruction. For pure hitting, though, Simmons was the best catcher I ever saw. He was an excellent switch hitter. He had no speed so he got no infield hits.

And he loved pressure situations. He wanted to be at the plate with the game on the line.

In the American League, I absolutely hate to face George Brett with the game on the line. I walk him an awful lot, too. But if there's no place to put him, then forget it. It's all over.

Guys like Mark McGwire and Jose Canseco can hurt you. But they're free swingers. They can be pitched to. Brett's different. He's got two swings. One is for power. When he knows he's in a situation where he must go deep, he's swinging so hard his shoe laces pop. But if he needs a hit, he shortens up and rips. Somehow the ball always finds a hole.

I do not want George Brett involved in any game in the ninth inning. In a 1983 game at Tiger Stadium, Brett had already hit two home runs before he came to bat in the ninth. I brought in a left-hander just to face him. It didn't matter. Brett blasted another one to beat us and the crowd booed me like it was New Year's Eve.

Don Mattingly is a lot like Brett. He hits for average and power. Mattingly showed me what he's made of on the last day of the 1984 season, which the Yankees finished against us. Mattingly was fighting Winfield for the batting title. Mattingly went out and proceeded to hit four straight ropes for hits. He beat Winfield, .343 to .340, for the title. He took charge. That's Don Mattingly.

The guy who has come on so strong the last couple of years is Kirby Puckett. When you add up power and total hits, he might be the best all-around hitter we have today. Puckett will be in the batting title race every year. He gets credit for destruction, too, because you know he's going to get twenty to thirty home runs every year. Puckett has that built-in alarm clock inside of him. It starts to ring when it's time to go home. He plays hard every inning. But when it's time to go home and you give him a chance to beat you, he'll oblige.

There are a lot more clutch players. Wade Boggs, Alan Trammell, Kent Hrbek, Gary Gaetti. These are guys who have impact on the field with the game on the line.

It takes something really special, though, to have impact with the fans. Of all the guys I've seen play, I'd always pay to see Rose, Bench, and Morgan. Rose was Rose. He's in a class by himself. Bench was the best ever at his position. And Morgan was so exciting, he could dominate a game.

I'd always pay to see McCovey. You just never knew if he was going to smack one into the ocean or if one of his line drives might kill someone.

I'd always pay to see Roberto Clemente. He was an artist. I'd always pay to see Ozzie Smith play shortstop. He's Harry Houdini with a glove.

When it comes to pitching, the most awesome creature I ever saw on a mound was J. R. Richard. But only for a given night. It wasn't all the time. Three out of four times, you had a chance to whip him. On that given night, when everything was going for him, there was no chance. Not for nobody.

He threw his fastball consistently around ninety-five and it sailed. Then he notched down on his slider and dropped it to about ninety. Morgan came back to the bench once and said; "I haven't ever seen anybody drop a slider to ninety."

He was six foot seven. He'd look in at you and start corkscrewing his hat to let you know who was out there. He was telling you not to get any fancy ideas. We had a great lineup. But when J.R. was on, we'd take our two hits, go home and be happy we didn't have to face him for another few weeks.

Richard could do it only on special nights. Bob Gibson could do it almost at will.

If you were going to war, you wanted Gibson on your side. He was one of those guys who could rise to the occasion. When he was pitching, San Diego and Montreal weren't good clubs. I'd watch the box scores when he pitched against them. He'd beat them, but he'd get hit a little. That was not the real Bob Gibson.

I watched the St. Louis pitching rotation to see when he was scheduled to start against us. I knew what was coming.

When he went up against a good team, it looked as if he threw his hat out on the mound and said, "Well boys, tonight you see the big guy. The big guy's going to do the talking tonight. You just sit back and watch."

That's the way he was. He could dominate you. It looked like he could turn it on whenever he pleased. When he was up against a good club like ours, he wanted to prove just who the best really was. It was as if he were saying, "You're good, boys . . . but I'm just a little bit better. Now what are you going to do about it?"

Gibson was a tremendous competitor. Nobody said a word to him when he was on the field. Because if they did, they might not live until the next day to talk about what they did say.

He wasn't going to bother anybody—unless he got bothered first. Just leave him alone and let him have his good nights. Don't be bothering with him. Don't be yelling at him or somebody's going to pay for it.

He didn't bother anyone and he didn't want to be bothered. He was conducting business. All he wanted to do was to stick the bat in somebody's ear till it came out the other side.

All the great ones have talent. That's a given. They all have class. Above all else, though, they all have pride. All of them have a burning desire to be the best.

It's not only for the money. All the great ones have great egos. They know they're the best and they want to show you who is the best. They never ask you to say how good they are. They don't need that. They'll show you.

They love being the best and they'll show you by the way they perform. You can't perform at the level these people perform without the greatest pride in the world. And that's the best thing a man can have.

The greatest ego trip in the world is being able to show people who pay their hard-earned money why they paid that money. The great ones make them want to come back and spend even more.

There's a sense of showmanship in all of them. It doesn't matter if it's the baseball diamond, the football field, or the basketball court. They're all on a stage. The great ones orchestrate how good the show will be. When the great one goes to bat, nobody wants to miss him. He's the one with *impact*.

Peter Edward Rose

When I managed my first year at Cincinnati in 1970 I was only thirty-six years old. I was the youngest manager in the league and there were plenty of players who were older than I was. At that time, Pete Rose had been with Cincinnati for seven full seasons. He was twenty-nine.

I remember my first spring training. One day Pete walked up to me.

"I make the most money around here," Pete said. "If you need anything done, you come to me."

He wasn't bragging. He wasn't joking, either. He was dead serious. Pete was telling the truth. That's the way he was. If he told you he'd get something done, you could go to the bank on it.

"Let me remind you if you're thinking about calling a team meeting, which I think you probably are," Pete would say when we were scuffling a little, "you remember to rip me. If you rip me, the rest of the guys will listen up. I can take it."

Pete could take that and everything two armies could throw at him. Pete could tackle anything that was thrown in front of him and not flinch for a second. Not once.

Peter Edward Rose is the toughest man I ever met in my life. I don't mean, just physically tough. I mean mentally tough. He's not a rock. He's a mountain.

There's one way to whip that man. That's to call up the coroner and have Rose pronounced dead. Make sure that coroner knows what he's doing, though, because if Rose is breathing, you're in trouble.

That's the best way I can describe Peter Edward Rose. That's the finest compliment I can give him.

I always used to joke with Pete and say, "Pete, you could murder someone, wait for the cops to show up, and then ask for two and a half hours to play one more game before they come back to get you." That was only a joke, but that's how tough this man is. He is so strong—physically and mentally—that he can overcome anything. You ain't never seen nobody as driven as Peter Edward Rose when he sets a goal for himself.

He wanted to get 4,000 hits. I thought it was impossible. So did everyone else on this planet. Pete got them. He played six years—at least six—more than I thought he could have played. That's because he drove himself so hard. He drove himself past the point at which every other human being would have thrown up his hands and quit.

I never saw a man who worked as hard as Pete did in spring training. He'd start off wearing a T-shirt, a sweatshirt, one of those rubber shirts that makes you sweat, and the regular uniform shirt. He had so much stuff on he looked like a walking closet. He did that so that he could sweat and really work his way down to the bone. By the end of the day when everyone else had gone,

Pete would still be out there taking batting practice with nothing but his T-shirt on. Man, it was soaking wet. He felt he had to do this.

All that work made him so strong, it was unbelievable. He never lifted a weight in his life. He was so strong that when he grabbed your hand, you thought it was in a vise. All that strength came from hard work and swinging the bat. Every single day in spring training after everyone was through, we had to give him fifteen minutes of right-handed pitching and fifteen minutes of left-handed pitching.

That sounds easy. But swinging a bat for thirty minutes straight after a workout is a workout itself. Most guys wouldn't be able to lift their arms after that. He did it for one reason. He was thinking about August.

"Wait till August and September come around," he said, "Those pitchers are going to be a little tired. Ol' Pete will still be there and his hands are going to be quick."

That didn't stop with spring training. Sometimes during the season if he had a bad night, he'd stay after the game to take extra batting practice. In my nine years at Cincinnati, I bet we had to keep the lights on for Pete after a game at least ten times. He put his jacket on and went back out there to hit.

There were no off-days for Pete. Every off-day he was at the park. We had to get a pitcher out there to throw to him. He could not take a day off from hitting. He had to hit every day.

I used to tell all the kids in spring training to watch Pete Rose.

"Just hang around and watch everything he does and then try to come as close as you can to him," I told them. "You'll have an outstanding career."

He had so much drive in him, he always thought he was eighteen years old. He never wanted to be more than eighteen.

Pete was good working with the young players. If any of them asked about hitting, he talked to them all day.

Pete also was good with young players in another way. Somehow he sensed when they felt awkward and out of place. Pete always knew the importance of a team feeling like a family and functioning as a single unit instead of a bunch of individuals running around in all different directions.

When a new player would come up and make the team out of spring training, Pete always had that youngster stay at his house in Cincinnati until he could find a home or apartment of his own. Pete would take him under his wing. He'd take that young man to dinner and make sure he started his big league career on the right foot.

Looking back, I made one of my best personnel moves the first year I got the job in Cincinnati in 1970 by naming Pete the team captain. He was a hometown boy and had the reputation of being "Charlie Hustle." That put the right guy on my side right from the start.

I never gave him the authority to talk to other players, but he put in his two cents worth when he thought it was necessary. He knew how to get on the guys in the right way. And if there was one thing another player didn't want it was to have Pete Rose harping on his case.

He joked with me about the move for a long time.

"I figured out right away that you were a smart man when you named me captain," he cracked.

He played harder than any man that ever put on a pair of spikes. Just because of that, I knew he had to be hurting on certain days. But he never wanted to be out of the lineup. In my nine years there, he missed a total of eight games. He couldn't understand how some guys wanted to get out of the lineup because they had a little injury. He used to call them "little boo-boos." It got him mad. I think it made him play even a little harder.

"What's a little pain?" he used to say. "Pain is in the mind. It's what you make of it."

I broke his consecutive game string once by sitting him down in the second game of a doubleheader. I felt he needed the rest and it would do more good for him to take a breather than to go out there to play like a runaway train for the second time that day.

Pete was upset. He didn't make a big scene with a name-calling argument, but he made his point. He stood way up in front of the dugout when the players took the field so the crowd could see him and wonder why he wasn't playing.

"Would you sit down here so we can get on with the game," I told him.

He cracked a grin and looked at me.

"No, I want them to see me," he said. "I want them to give you a good old-fashioned razzing."

That's the way he was every single day of his entire career. I've seen guys who can compete like there's no tomorrow for a week or two . . . maybe even a couple of months.

Pete did it for 162 games a year! And he did it year after year after year.

Pete never gave away one time at bat. It didn't matter what the score was. We could be up by nine runs or down by nine when one more hit wouldn't make a difference either way. He batted as if the score were tied in the bottom of the ninth.

If he had two hits that day, he wanted three. If he had three, he wanted four.

"I might need that extra hit," he used to say. "Tomorrow I might not get any."

When he was at the plate, nothing in the world could distract him. He wanted that pitcher. He wanted to show him nobody was better than him.

Pete knew the strike zone better than anybody in the world. He could tell if the pitch was a quarter inch off the plate either way. His eyesight was incredible. He could pick up the spin of the pitch as soon as the ball left the pitcher's hand.

Now here's the amazing part. Pete did all this without any ability. The man didn't really have any tools at all. He wasn't a fast runner. He wasn't a good thrower. He wasn't a great fielder. He didn't have that much power. Yet the man could beat you in more ways than any other player I ever played with or against.

They say Ty Cobb was like that. I don't know. I never saw him play. But I can't believe anybody ever played with more enthusiasm or drive than Peter Edward Rose. He had that burning desire to perform beyond all the real ability he had. That's why I admire the man as the single greatest player ever to live. He took ordinary talent all the way to Hall of Fame results. He took it beyond all imagination. No man ever will accomplish what Pete did. No man ever will come close to 4,000 hits again.

He ran right over players. If he was going into second base and the second baseman was in the way, that man wound up in left field. That's the way the game is supposed to be played according to Pete. He expected the same thing if the roles were reversed.

He took out Ray Fosse at the plate in the 1970 All-Star Game. Fosse was injured so badly that he never played much after that. Pete didn't try to hurt him. The game didn't really mean that much. But it was the winning run and Pete had to score it.

I remember a game against St. Louis during the mid-seventies. A pitcher named Alan Foster knocked Pete down. I don't know how the pitch missed his head. I thought Pete was dead.

Pete jumped up madder than a bull that lost his horns. He drilled the next pitch over the left center field fence. While he was circling the bases he called that pitcher every name you could imagine and some we hadn't even heard before. When he got to home plate he took off at the catcher—Ted Simmons—and then looked back at Foster and started to yell at him all over again. That pitcher never once took a step toward Pete. We were all glad because Pete would have destroyed him.

Pete never meant any harm. To him, that was the way the game is played.

The 1973 playoff incident between Pete and Bud Harrelson at Shea Stadium is a classic example of Pete's approach to the game and to life.

We were getting our brains knocked 9–2, and everyone figured the game was over.

Everyone but Pete, that is. Like I said, he's got to be dead before it's over for him.

Pete was on first when Joe Morgan hit a grounder to John Milner at first base. Milner fired the ball to second for one out and Harrelson relayed back to first for the double play.

Now the action really began.

Pete had crashed into Harrelson like Dick Butkus used to crack into ball carriers. Harrelson apparently said something to Pete and his reply was a shove to the face.

They started at it and pretty soon both benches cleared. When the dust had settled the fans decided to get into the act. When Pete got to his position in left field, those New York fans pelted him with every piece of garbage that wasn't in a trash can. I pulled my team off the field and some Mets players were asked to go out to left field to ask the fans to let the game finish.

They did and the Mets won, 9–2. The next day the incident was the headline in every newspaper.

"I knocked the war in the Middle East right off the front pages of the New York papers," Rose quipped.

Pete never admitted it, but I believe to this day that he did what he did to Harrelson to stir up the team. He felt our team was getting a little lax and he was trying to spark a fire in us.

The next day the crowd booed Pete like Hitler was in the lineup. But Pete got the last laugh.

Trailing 1–0, Tony Perez tied the game with a solo home run in the eighth inning.

In the twelfth, Pete popped a solo shot and we won the game 2–1.

I'll never forget the way one New York writer described that home-run scene: "It was a sight to see the man running the bases. Pete was an emperor returning in triumph from the wars to his Capital City. He was the heavyweight champion of the world. He was an Olympic hero breasting the tape. As he ran, he held his right arm high, his fist clenched. And there wasn't a soul in the park who didn't understand, even though the Mets had a time at bat left, that this was it."

Pete has never known the meaning of pressure. He used to laugh at guys when he heard that word.

"How can you be afraid?" he used to say. "Afraid of what? What can possibly beat you if you want to win hard enough? Pressure is for sissies."

The man played for the fans. He gave the public the best game he could play every day of his life. He never cheated the crowd. He believed the crowd came to see him. They paid their way into the park to see him perform. They didn't spend their money to see the other guys. They came to watch Pete Rose.

That's the way he thought. And he couldn't let the fans down. Even on his bad days, he gave the fans all he had.

That's the way he attacked life. He never looked behind him or even to the side. It was straight ahead. If there's a fight, let's go for it. If there's a problem, let's tackle it. That's the way Pete was raised. He learned it in the streets. Pete is the smartest street person I've ever known.

He always used to say that's where you learn life. It doesn't happen in a book. It happens out on the street with the people.

He competed in everything. I'm no expert in this field, but that's why it doesn't surprise me that he did wager on football and basketball games. That was just an extension of his competitiveness.

With Pete, it's always Rose against another player or Rose against another manager. Pete has to be part of the action. So if there's a football game or basketball game he's interested in, making that wager gives him part of the action.

To be around Pete Rose even for a year is a pleasure. I called him "The Animal." I saw a man compete like no one ever imagined a human being could compete. He takes no quarters and gives no quarters. In fact, if he had one of those steamrollers used to pave roads, he'd run right over you and not worry about it. He expects the same from you. That's the way he plays the game of baseball. That's the way he plays the game of life. Pete simply has to compete. He is not a spectator. He has to be a player. That's the competitiveness in the man.

What happened to Rose in 1989 when he was banned from baseball is a tragedy. It's a tragedy because I don't think a man of his stature and greatness with all that he means to this game and all of its fans should be involved with something like that. But it happened. And the greatest thing about the tragic affair is that he was never proven guilty of betting on baseball games. That's the part I like.

A lot of people can claim that he did. Pete said he didn't. The agreement between the commissioner and Rose was that it would be dropped.

So I honestly don't know if Pete did bet on baseball. Nobody else honestly knows. Everyone is entitled to their opinion. But that opinion is all they really have.

Pete denies he bet on baseball. So only Pete and God really know for sure. That's the way it should be. We have no right to judge another man. If he did bet on baseball, then Pete's the one who has to live with it. If he didn't, then he's free.

But only Pete and God know for sure.

What pleased me was that the affair was settled by the commissioner of baseball. It was not settled in court. It bothered me a lot when it looked like it might be settled in court. I definitely did not want that to happen. I believe every decision in our game must be made by the commissioner. Right or wrong he must rule. If he happens to be wrong, that's something we must accept. He is the commissioner and he must rule the game.

I never had the opportunity to meet Bart Giammati. I'm sorry I didn't. Watching that man I believe all of us in baseball and all of the game's fans suffered an enormous loss with his death. I think we lost the chance to realize the emergence of another Judge Landis. I think we may have lost what could have been the greatest commissioner in the history of baseball.

The tragedy is that he never really got the chance to become the man he was destined to be. He only passed through base-ball long enough for a cup of coffee. But his greatness was obvious.

The way he handled Rose's case was a piece of art. We're only starting to realize now just how beautifully Giammati put every-thing together. A lot of people in baseball—myself included—would have rushed to make a decision so as to look like the knight in shining armor.

Giammati didn't. He didn't want to be a star. He didn't need it. He was patient, he was thorough, and he was wise. He loved baseball so much he felt he had to do everything in his power to make his decision 100 percent correct. And that's exactly what he did.

He had three things in mind. First, he had to keep the game and its credibility intact. Above all, the game must be upheld. No one man is bigger than the game. Giammati upheld the game's integrity in the way he handled the case. Baseball was not blem-ished.

Second, he felt he had to keep the commissioner's power intact. He did that splendidly by getting the job done himself without the courts making the final decision.

And third, he felt he must honor and respect one of the game's greatest players. Giammati loved baseball. It was his passion. Don't think for even a second that it didn't pain him to do what he had to do to a man like Pete Rose. That's why he did every-thing so carefully and with so much dignity. Rose deserved that; Giammati recognized that.

Giammati was a tremendously intelligent man with an incred-ible amount of sensitivity for baseball. That's why he agonized so much and worked so hard on the case. But I honestly don't believe that the Rose case had anything to do with Giammati's death. Any man who held that position and was as wise as Giammati was certainly strong enough to deal with any kind of pressure. Anyone who would dream of laying the blame on Rose for Giammati's death has to be set straight.

Eventually I believe Pete will realize that Giammati did care about him. He cared about Rose more than anybody realized. He maneuvered the whole affair to protect the game's integrity, protect the office of the commissioner, and protect Rose. I believe after Pete truly studies the situation he'll understand what that man did. He'll appreciate him the rest of his life. Because Pete Rose loves baseball.

That's why nothing in the whole affair changed my thinking on Pete one bit. In fact, I was amazed the way he handled himself throughout the whole ordeal. To manage a ball club from spring training through August with the pressure he had to endure day after day took a Superman. It took a Pete Rose.

Rose has to be in the Hall of Fame. The mistake that's being made is not putting him in the Hall right now. I don't understand the five-year waiting rule when it comes to a man like Rose.

Wait for what? His credentials aren't going to change. He did things no other person ever will come close to doing again.

The voting should be judged on what a player did on the field. Whatever he did off the field, only God should judge. There's no other way. If we had to vote on the personal life of every person in the Hall of Fame there might be a lot of plaques missing.

Let's not talk about somebody's personal life. That has nothing to do with nothing. And besides, it wasn't proven that Pete did bet on baseball.

Peter Edward Rose is a once-in-a-lifetime piece of work. There'll never be another one. Our game will never be blessed with another player like him. He's the last of the great performers who could grind it out for 162 games a year.

He believes more in himself than any man I've ever been around. He drove himself as hard as a human being could possibly drive himself. He proved one thing to every child all over the world. If you've got a dream and you're willing to drive that dream as hard as you can drive it, then you can reach it.

I admire him more than anyone I've ever been around because

he should never have attained the greatness that he did. He attained it through sheer determination. It's a tremendous tribute to say that he really did not have that much talent.

But he had desire. No one will ever have it like Peter Edward Rose.

All-Timers

I'm no different than anyone else when it comes to picking favorite players. I love it. I might have different reasons for my choices than the fans do, but I still have my favorites.

I don't like to go just by the numbers. The record book helps but I prefer picking my all-time team from the players I've seen. I know firsthand what these guys have done. They've either done it for me or done it to me. Either way, I respect them.

I've been lucky to see many great players. Picking an all-time team means some awfully good players are left out and I mean no disrespect. But I believe this team could play with anybody from any period in history.

FIRST BASE—WILLIE MCCOVEY

The most fearsome power hitter I ever saw in my career. He was as good as Babe Ruth or Lou Gehrig or any of the immortals were. I'll never believe anyone ever hit the ball harder than Willie Mac. He was six-four and all muscle. A lethal weapon at the plate.

He once hit a shot at our first baseman, Lee May. I thought May was dead. May never had a chance to put his hands up. It was hit that hard. The ball just cleared his head and wound up smashing off the right field fence. If it had hit May in the face, he would have been a goner.

Willie Mac finished with 521 home runs and he never played in a home-run park. If he had played in Atlanta, Detroit, Seattle, or Minnesota, he would have hit 700. It wouldn't have been safe for people walking down the street behind the right field stands.

I swear one time he hit a ball into San Francisco Bay. That was before they had those stands out there in right field in Candlestick Park. He crushed the ball and it just disappeared into the darkness. Boom . . . it was gone! We waited for the splash but couldn't hear it.

I walked this man more times than any other batter. He used to call me "Mr. Four." That's because he was so used to seeing me hold up four fingers to my pitcher to give him a walk.

He'd see me on the field before a game and hold up four fingers.

"And how are you today?" he'd say to me.

He never said a word about anything. He never complained about being walked all the time until a game in 1971. The Giants were fighting for the pennant with a week to go and were playing in our park. We were out of it, but we'd just beaten the Dodgers three in a row and now we'd taken two straight from the Giants.

I walked Willie Mac one more time in the third game. As he

192

started down to first base, he screamed at me: "Who do you think I am—Babe Ruth?"

I didn't care. I didn't say anything. But Alex Grammas who was standing next to me in the dugout yelled out, "You're better!"

The roles were reversed the next year and I gave Willie Mac his shot. We had just clinched the division in Los Angeles before going up to San Francisco for three games. Before the first game, he came up to me.

"Now you guys already have the division in your pocket," Willie Mac said. "So please do me a favor and pitch to me all day."

"Okay," I said. "But when they come to put me in a straitjacket and cart me away, you'll know the reason why."

Well, we pitched to him. The second time up he knocked a fastball halfway to the Golden Gate Bridge. When he trotted past our dugout while circling the bases, he looked at me sheepishly.

Next day during batting practice I walked straight up to him.

"Now do you finally know why I hold up four fingers when you come to bat?" I asked him.

We both had a good laugh.

SECOND BASE—JOE MORGAN

It ain't even close. I don't know of another player I ever managed that could beat you offensively so many ways. He was the greatest all around offensive player I ever managed. I never saw a man have four years in a row like he had for Cincinnati in the early seventies.

He averaged more than .300. He averaged more than 20 homers and 90 RBIs a year. He averaged more than 100 runs and 30 doubles. He averaged more than 60 stolen bases, and he never stole a single base when it didn't mean something.

He refused to do it. He ran on his own, but he wouldn't attempt to steal unless it affected the game. It was against his nature.

In Game Seven of the 1975 World Series at Boston, Bill Lee threw over to first base thirteen straight times to hold Morgan close. On the fourteenth throw, he was halfway down to second and stole the base with ease. He could read a pitcher like he was reading a newspaper.

He is the only player I've ever been around where, if the game was tied in the ninth or extra innings and he was leading off, you knew you had it won. He'd hit a home run or get on base some way. Then he'd steal second, we'd bunt him to third, and it was over.

Of all the clutch hits he ever delivered, I remember best his game-winning single in the ninth inning of that seventh game in 1975 to snap a 3–3 tie. It wasn't a shot. It was more of a flare to center. But he got the job done as he always did.

Morgan won two MVP Awards in that four-year span and easily could have won four straight. No one could have argued if he had.

The only thing he couldn't do in the field was throw. If he could have thrown, he would have been the greatest second baseman of all time. He had the rest of it—quick hands and quick feet. He could dive, stop a ball, and be back on his feet so quick throwing you couldn't believe your eyes.

We used to tease him about his arm. When he'd relay the ball to first base for a double play, we'd all stand on the dugout steps and try to suck the air out of the stadium so the ball would get there faster.

He knew we were kidding. He took it professionally because he was a tremendous pro. He had the greatest instincts as a player I ever saw. He was a manager on the field.

THIRD BASE—WADE BOGGS AND GEORGE BRETT

I have to make it a tie. Give me either one and I'll be happy. They've got two different styles.

With Boggs, before the season starts, you write down .350 with 100 walks and 100 runs. Whatever he gets above that is a bonus. But you know what to bank on before even starting.

That man does so much for the Boston lineup it's incredible. He sets the table for all those bruisers. He's on base one way or another all the time. It's impossible to get a third strike past him. He's got uncanny eyes. With Boggs up, a runner on third and less than two out is like money in the bank. That man scores.

With Brett you get .320, but he pops the ball out of the park a few times.

Brett is one of the greatest hitters of our time. He plays situations really well. If the situation calls for a hit, he's got that one swing that makes sure to make contact with the ball. If the situation is late in a game and the long ball is needed, he's got that home run swing.

Pitch him inside and he drills it to right. Pitch him away and he drives it to left.

Before injuries forced him to move to first base, Brett worked tirelessly at making himself a good third baseman. Boggs has done the same thing. Now he's one of the best third basemen in the league.

I'll take either one.

SHORTSTOP—ALAN TRAMMELL

I've seen some great shortstops—Dave Concepcion, Ozzie Smith, and Cal Ripken, just to name a few.

I'll take Trammell because of everything he can do. Smith is a wizard in the field and can do more with the glove. Ripken is stronger and hits with more power. But Trammell does everything.

Trammell hits 15 homers a year, knocks in 90 runs a year and always plays around the .300 mark. In the field he never botches a routine play. People take that for granted, but that's the sign of a great shortstop. If he gets a ground ball, it's an out.

I've seen Trammell carry us in a pennant race after we lost a couple of key people like Lance Parrish and Kirk Gibson. That takes a special kind of player.

In 1987, we had no business winning the East Division title. A big chunk of the credit belongs to Trammell.

Trammell is not a home-run hitter. Because we were desperate for a cleanup hitter, I had to put Tram there, and he came through all year long. He finished with 28 homers and 105 RBIs. When it got down to nitty-gritty time in September, Tram was there. He batted .416 for the month and knocked in 17 runs. We won the division on the last day of the season.

I've watched this man for eleven years. I saw him when he earned $50,000 a year and now when he earns $2 million a year and he hasn't changed one bit. That's remarkable. That's the sign of a true pro.

OUTFIELD—ROBERTO CLEMENTE, WILLIE STARGELL, AND HANK AARON

Walking away . . . Clemente is my premier outfielder. Period.

People tell me Willie Mays was the best outfielder that ever lived, but I never saw him in his prime. I never saw Willie Mays when he really was Willie Mays.

I saw more of Clemente than I wanted to when I managed against him. The man could hit for power when he had to. When he wanted to slap it to right, he shot the ball like a bullet.

Plus he could fly. When he hit a ground ball to the infield, he was flying to first. That fielder better not be napping.

Clemente was a remarkable man because at the ages of thirty-four and thirty-five, he played like he was twenty-one years old. I never saw anything like it.

196

I remember once when the Pirates came to Cincinnati for a five-game series in four days. Clemente wasn't in the lineup for any of the games. Believe me, that didn't bother me to have him out of there. But I was curious so I questioned Danny Murtaugh, the Pirate manager.

"He's been very tired," Murtaugh said. "He's been resting. But watch what happens next week and the rest of the season."

I checked the box scores every day. There was Clemente . . . three hits, two hits, three hits, four hits, two hits, day after day. Clemente came back and led the Pirates to the pennant. The man got tired just like everybody else. But once he was rested, he was like a kid again. That's how I'll always remember him—as a man who played with youthful energy.

Stargell was different. People don't realize how much power Stargell had. All around the National League parks there are marks way up in the upper decks where he hit balls. When I went around the league I'd stare at some of those marks and say there ain't no way possible a human being could have done that. But he did. And this is every park, not just one or two. I saw Stargell hit a ball off Clay Kirby in the old Pittsburgh ballpark before they moved to Three Rivers Stadium that actually knocked off the back of a seat. None of us could believe what we saw because that seat was way out in right center field. The thing actually cracked in half.

You could get Stargell to chase a few bad pitches. But he was a better hitter than people realized. He was a tough out, especially when the game was on the line.

The best thing about Stargell was his influence on his club and the teams he played against. He was gentle as a lamb. He made you feel good to be around him. But he was an intimidator. He didn't have to say anything. He knew it.

He was so imposing when he walked up to the plate. That was part of his game plan. He walked really slowly. He made sure that pitcher knew what he was getting himself into.

Aaron was the opposite. He didn't look that big. He didn't look like an intimidator. He simply left death and destruction when he was finished.

He was the quietest player I ever saw. He never said a word. He just showed up for work and played hard every day.

If the game was on the line, you were in trouble. He'd do it to you quietly and efficiently. Because it was him, it almost didn't hurt. How could you get upset at a player like Aaron?

Aaron was strong. He had those lightning-quick wrists. A pitcher thought he had the ball by him and then Aaron would flick those wrists to send a ball up the gap. I swear he was able to pick a ball out of the catcher's mitt.

Everybody knows Aaron finished with the most home runs and most RBIs in history. What they forget is that he also batted .305 and could steal a base whenever he wanted. One year he stole 31 bases. He finished his career with 240.

The amazing thing is that Aaron never hit more than forty-seven homers in one season. That's a tremendous tribute in my opinion. It shows how consistent he was.

CATCHER—JOHNNY BENCH

Johnny Bench is the best catcher I ever saw. I'll go one better than that.

Casey Stengel said Bench was the best he ever saw and Casey saw all of them, including Bill Dickey and Yogi Berra! Casey said no one could do all the things Bench did. I saw all those things every day and still can't believe them.

Bench was a catcher with the batting stats of an outfielder. For catchers, he's the all-time leader in home runs and RBIs. He had so much power he looked like a man playing against little boys.

He did more than hit home runs. He could shoot the ball to right field when he had to. I used to hit-and-run with him all the time.

If I had to pick one player who played his position better than anyone else, I'd pick Bench. Whatever you'd see him do on the field, you'd never see again till he did it again.

Everyone marveled at his arm. It was a cannon but others threw harder. What made him so deadly were his quick feet. He got into position to throw faster than a dancer. If he was in a throwing contest, Bench would have the ball on its way to second while the other guys were just cocking their arms.

It's really difficult for me to talk about Johnny Bench because we may be talking about the best man in his position in the history of the game. I can't dream there could be anyone better.

John also is a brilliant man. He knows how to handle himself in every type of situation. John is extremely talented at doing TV commercials. After Mark Spitz won all those medals in the Olympics, some advertiser flew John to Los Angeles to help Spitz learn how to do them.

Bench is from Oklahoma City, Oklahoma, and he owns that state. I always said Johnny Bench could be elected governor of Oklahoma—and he'd run the state well.

ANYWHERE—PETER EDWARD ROSE

I don't care where you put him. Peter Edward must be on the team. Here's a guy who didn't have enough talent to be a good first baseman, second baseman, third baseman, or outfielder. Yet he made the All-Star Team at all those positions.

Nobody who ever put on a uniform ever played the game harder than Peter Edward Rose. Nobody will ever top his record of 4,256 hits.

He could beat you in so many ways, it was unbelievable. He simply knew how to win.

I told every kid who ever came into camp the same thing; "Follow Pete Rose and do what he does. If you do that, you'll never have a problem with baseball in your whole career."

No man I know ever kept his mental toughness for 162 games

the way Peter Edward Rose did. And he did it for more than twenty years. He never wasted one time at bat.

If he had two hits, he wanted three. If he had three, he wanted four. We could be down by ten runs late in a game and Rose would scrap as hard for a hit then as when the score was tied.

I asked him about that once.

"I might not get a hit tomorrow," he said. "So every one I get today makes a difference in the long run."

Peter Edward Rose is the greatest single example for young players that I've ever known. Only in America could you not have the ability to be a major leaguer—and he didn't have it at the beginning—and still be a shoo-in for the Hall of Fame.

STARTING PITCHERS— SANDY KOUFAX, BOB GIBSON, AND JUAN MARICHAL

Sandy Koufax was totally overpowering. His fastball started at the batter's belly. By the time the batter swung, it was up at his shoulder. It shot up like there was a spring in it.

He had the best curveball I ever saw. It fell straight down. It looked like there was an anchor in it. He started it shoulder high. When it finished it was at the hitter's knees. You couldn't hit it if he told you it was coming.

Koufax was the only pitcher I ever saw who, for a five-year period, was totally above the major leagues. He actually was in a league all by himself. There were the minor leagues, the major leagues, and Sandy Koufax.

One night we were playing in the Los Angeles Coliseum and Wally Post struck out four times against him. There were two out in the ninth and Post was on deck. The batter lined one off that big screen in left. He had no right to go for it, but he tried for a double and was thrown out by a mile.

As we were going up the runway to the clubhouse, Post said to me; "Bless his heart . . . I was about to tie the record."

Gibson was the master intimidator. On a given night, if he

chose to embarrass you, he could make your face redder than a fire engine. There was no way to hit him.

He threw hard and harder. He took no nonsense. He was all business on the mound. He'd move a batter back off the plate if he dug in too much. He wouldn't hit the batter. He didn't have to.

What amazed me was the way he always pitched better when he pitched against good teams. That proved he was a tremendous competitor.

A man can't pitch three hundred innings in one year. A man can't strike out three hundred hitters in one year. A man can't have a 1.12 ERA in one year.

Bob Gibson did all of those. He was totally awesome. At times he was totally unhittable. He was an athlete in the true sense of the word. He could have played any position on the field and played it well. He played basketball for the Harlem Globetrotters and probably could have played any professional sport if he put his mind to it.

Marichal was the complete artist. God didn't give him the power arm that Koufax and Gibson had. So Marichal had to paint a picture on the mound. Marichal would show you three different curveballs. He'd show you three different change-ups. He'd throw you an impossibly twisting screwball. Then he'd spot that little eighty-five-mile-an-hour fastball whenever he wanted and it looked like it was going more than one hundred.

Koufax and Gibson almost yelled out, "Here it comes . . . hit me if you can." Every time out they flirted with a no-hitter. You always wondered if tonight was going to be the night. With Marichal, the hitters just tried not to be embarrassed. He knew how to tease before putting in the stinger.

RELIEVER—ROLLIE FINGERS

Rollie Fingers is the only one. He's the greatest reliever of all time. There have been a lot of good ones, but no one will match Fingers.

It's not because of his 113 wins and 324 saves. It's because he was ready to take the ball every day and he was never scared.

We once beat him three days in a row in Cincinnati. He came into three tie games and we got the winning run off him all three times.

I checked the box scores as soon as he left and for the next week he kept picking up save after save.

The next time I saw him in San Diego I asked him how he could bounce back like that.

"It's simple," he said. "When I come into the game, I'm going to attack you. The batter is going to attack me. I don't worry about it.

"If the hitter gets me one night, good for him. I'll be back the next night and I'll get him. Why worry about it? What happens, happens. I'm coming back the next day and you better be ready."

All the good ones have outstanding stuff. The great ones never run scared.

Defense is a critical part of the game that often gets overlooked. Not in my book. Here's my all-time defensive team.

FIRST BASE—WES PARKER

First base is a position that gets passed over too easily. Some people think anybody can play first. All the guy has to do is stick up his glove. There's a big difference. You've never seen a great infield that didn't have a good first baseman.

Wes Parker was the best. He was like having an extra man out there. If the throw was within radar distance, Parker caught it. Every infielder he played with had a better arm because of him. He caught throws other first basemen couldn't handle.

He dug throws out of the dirt and got to balls hit on either side. He had great range. When he had to throw, it was like an arrow.

202

There was nothing he couldn't do with a glove. He played tricks with it.

SECOND BASE—BILL MAZEROSKI

Bill Mazeroski was a machine. I honestly believe somebody wound him up before games and programmed him to catch anything hit that stayed in the same area code.

If Mazeroski had played his whole career on Astroturf, he never would have made an error.

He turned the double play so fast, you never saw the ball touch his glove. He made the throw look like he was just reaching over to touch his shoulder. And there was fire on the throw.

THIRD BASE—DOUG RADER

I saw Doug Rader make so many great plays that I can't keep him off my team. He charged the bunt as if there were a million dollars in the ball. He guarded the line and still had enough range to help the shortstop in the hole. He had a strong arm and a true one.

I saw Brooks Robinson only in the World Series and All-Star Games. He was unbelievable. I saw Rader more and I never saw him miss.

SHORTSTOP—OZZIE SMITH

Ozzie Smith is the best defensive shortstop I've ever seen. The things he does with the glove and with his arm ought to be outlawed. They aren't human.

I've seen him throw from the outfield and get the runner at

first base by two steps. Harry Houdini couldn't do what Ozzie Smith does. I'd pay just to see Smith play shortstop.

RIGHT FIELD—ROBERTO CLEMENTE

Roberto Clemente wrote the book about playing right field. He made every play and he also knew how to trick you.

Preston Gomez warned me about that when I coached third base for him at San Diego in 1969. He told me to watch Clemente on a base hit to right with the runner rounding second.

Clemente would lope in after the ball. But the moment you started waving the runner over, he sprang into action. He watched out of the corner of his eye. He'd race in quickly, pick up the ball, and it would be waiting for the runner when he got to third. His arm was a laser.

I'd be standing in the coach's box watching my runner charging. Then I'd see the ball coming and I'd say, "Not again!" The ball won every time.

CENTER FIELD—PAUL BLAIR

I never saw Willie Mays in his prime. But I can't imagine how anyone could have played center better than Paul Blair. He had that instinct. It's something no player can learn. It has to be inside of him. Blair had it. That's why he was able to play so shallow on every hitter.

It almost looked as if he were daring every hitter to knock one over his head. He really wasn't. He just knew he could play there and make all the plays. Over his career, there's no telling how many hits he saved his pitchers by playing so shallow. In his quiet way, he contributed a great deal to the success of those great Baltimore teams.

LEFT FIELD—WILLIE WILSON

When Kansas City played Willie Wilson in left and Amos Otis in center, it was as if they had two center fielders at the same time. That outfield was covered like a blanket.

Wilson covered so much ground it was impossible to shoot the gap. He owned the line and wasn't afraid to go into the corner. He played the corner like a pool shark.

CATCHER—JOHNNY BENCH

There's nobody else you can mention with his name. You'd embarrass them and you'd embarrass Johnny Bench. When we got into a tight game, we never worried about the other team running on us. They had to hit the ball to beat us. Do you realize the edge that gave us over a 162-game season?

Bench was a one and only. No man will ever play his position as well as Bench played his. I don't mean just catcher. I mean any position.

At the end of the season we'd look at his gloves and they weren't worn except for the exact spot where he caught the ball. That's how good he was.

The fielders would never see the number on his back. That's because he never had to turn around to chase a ball to the backstop. Nothing got by him.

He was brilliant. He called an excellent game. He made the pitchers have confidence.

Why was Bench that good? There's only one reason. God touched his mother when he was born. He said, "I'm giving you the finest defensive player in the history of the game of baseball."

PITCHER—JACK MORRIS

Now and forever I don't think I'll ever see a pitcher as quick as Jack Morris. Don Gullett at Cincinnati was so quick he made hitters look silly going down the line, but Morris is quicker. He gets off the mound like a fifth infielder. He saves himself runs every year with his defense. He's a tremendous athlete. I'm sure that if he didn't pitch, he could be a position player.

Giants

I've always been interested in studying people even when I was a little kid growing up in South Dakota. I don't know what I thought I was looking at, but I was mesmerized by people. I watched how they walked and how they dressed. I listened to what they talked about even though I didn't understand everything they said.

I used to walk over to the bus station just to watch the people getting on and off. My mother always knew where to find me. If she needed me, she'd go to the baseball park or the bus station. I'd be standing there staring with my mouth wide open.

As I grew up I became fascinated by the giants of our society. These are people like Rockefeller, Kennedy, Trump, Iacocca: Just say the name and people know who you're talking about. You don't even have to mention the first name. One name says it all.

We use the word *legend* way too much. There simply aren't that many people who deserve it. But sports do provide fans with enough genuine legends. These are guys whose reputations stay with us long after they're gone. Their names are magic. When we hear them we become kids again.

I can't honestly say my managing has been influenced by the people I consider to be legends. I've learned from them. I've gained from their experiences and their accomplishments. But I've never tried to do something simply because someone else has.

When it comes strictly to managing, three people have had the most influence on me. The first was Lefty Phillips. As I said, I first met Lefty when I was fourteen years old and he was a part-time scout for Cincinnati. He taught me more about baseball than I could have learned from reading a library full of books on the game.

The second was Charlie Dressen who wound up managing in the big leagues for sixteen years. He taught me about pitching— what to watch for and what to protect against.

The most important lesson he taught me was never to take my eye off a pitcher from the time a game starts until it's over. If a pitcher starts throwing high in the first inning, don't get excited, he's just getting himself adjusted. If he's still throwing the ball high in the second inning, then you've got a problem. If he gets into a jam in the first inning and works his way out, that's fine. If he does it again in the fourth inning, no problem. But if he gets into another jam in the sixth inning, get him out of there. Never allow your pitcher to work his way out of three jams! It just doesn't work.

The third main influence on my managing was Clay Bryant. He was one of my managers when I played in the minor leagues. He taught me that you're not supposed to lose! Period.

These are my personal legends. They're the giants of my managing career. But I'm a fan like everyone else when it comes to sports. I've got favorites and there are guys I think are bums.

I'm fascinated by some of these people. I can't learn enough about them. I marvel at their accomplishments and the way they handle pressure, and it helps me forget about some of the pressures of my own job.

Baseball is a fertile field for producing legends. Baseball and boxing are the best for making names that live forever.

Some of these names go back to the turn of the century. It doesn't matter how old you are, these names command immediate recognition and respect.

THE BABE

Everybody knows Babe Ruth. A person might hate baseball, but he still knows The Babe was one of the greatest home-run hitters in history. Many people don't even know his real name was George Herman Ruth. But they know The Babe.

YOGI

Some people don't know his last name is Berra. Hardly anybody knows his real name is Lawrence Peter Berra. But everybody knows Yogi was that dumpy little catcher who hit a lot of home runs for the Yankees and said all those funny things.

MICKEY

There seem to be a lot of Mickeys now. Just say Mickey, though, and everybody thinks the same thing—Mickey Mantle. That name is magic. It's a baseball treasure.

DiMAGGIO

Some people know he hit in fifty-six straight games one year. Some people remember he married Marilyn Monroe. Some people know him as Mr. Coffee—the classy man with the distinguished white hair who pitches automatic coffee makers. Everybody knows Joe DiMaggio.

CASEY

My all-time favorite. When you say Casey, you don't even have to say Stengel. He was The Old Professor. The manager of all those great Yankee teams. He had the big nose, the stooped shoulders, and talked in circles. Casey was The Old Man.

ROSE

Peter Edward has fallen on some tough times. But we all remember him as the hitting machine who used to run through brick walls.

Baseball is special when it comes to legends. That's because we're bombarded by the media. Newspapers make players part of our everyday lives. Television makes them part of our families. We might not know all of their statistics or even what positions they play. But we know their names. The giants actually become bigger than life.

Boxing doesn't get the same everyday exposure that baseball enjoys, but the hype for a big championship fight is overwhelming. I've always been fascinated by the great boxers. Not just by what it takes physically, but what goes into their games psychologically. When you go into that ring, it's just you against the other guy. Make a mistake and you pay for it. Play it right and the gold is yours.

There's no teammate around to pick you up if you make an error. You're out there alone. One-on-one. Don't look over your shoulder for help because you ain't getting any. You do it or you die. You can't run scared, or else . . .

When I managed at Modesto in the California State League, we always had Mondays off. I'd drive up to Stockton every week to watch the fights.

One of the biggest thrills I've ever had in my life was in 1985 when I went to the Marvin Hagler–Tommy Hearns fight in Las Vegas. It was the first championship fight I ever went to. It was in April and we had an off-day. Tom Monaghan took Jim Campbell and me in his private jet just to see the fight.

I'd never seen such a spectacle. I never realized what a happening a championship fight is. It's more than a fight. It's a production. You've heard the expression "electricity in the air." There was more than electricity. There was dynamite.

Before the fight they introduced the former champions who were there. There was Muhammad Ali, Sugar Ray Leonard, Carmen Basilio, and Billy Conn. I looked around ringside and saw all of the beautiful people. There were diamonds, furs, and gold. It was a page out of a fashion magazine. I saw the original $6-million man—Lee Majors. And sitting directly opposite me across the ring was Bo Derek.

Before the fight, the Hearns people invited Monaghan and me into Tommy's dressing room. I always wondered what a fighter did before a big match. The locker room was packed with all his people. Just before he went out, they formed a giant circle around him. Tommy started to loosen up with some shadowboxing. They'd yell out "Hit Man" and Tommy would let loose with a flurry of punches.

I tried to imagine exactly what was going through his mind. I guess he tried to shut out everything except Hagler. But only Tommy knew for sure. I know one thing—it gozzled my mind.

My all-time personal hero was Joe Louis. He's the only person I had as an idol while I was growing up.

When I managed at Cincinnati one of those sports quiz TV programs had Pete Rose, Johnny Bench, Joe Morgan, and me on as panelists. They brought out a mystery guest who we couldn't see. After a few clues I figured out it was Joe Louis. When I realized it was him and I was going to have the opportunity to meet him, my heart started beating like a drum.

This was Joe Louis. This was The Man.

The one sports figure who had more influence on sports and society than anybody who ever lived is Muhammad Ali. No one else even comes close. For Ali, the words *legend* and *superstar* really don't fit. They're not enough. He's beyond all that. He's somewhere way out on another level. We were just blessed to see this man and experience his greatness as a boxer and as an entertainer.

It's not what Ali did during his career; it's how he did it. I'll guarantee no one will ever come close to doing it again. Muhammad Ali was not just a once-in-a-lifetime phenomenon. He was a once-in-history happening.

Ali not only had an impact on boxing. He not only had an impact on sports. His impact was on our whole society. And not just in the United States but all over the world.

He took heavyweight fights to Manila and Zaire. He was an international phenomenon. He once said he was better known around the world than the Pope. He didn't mean any disrespect. In fact, he probably was telling the truth.

Some people didn't respect Ali because of his religious beliefs or the politics he got into. What right do we have to look into another man's mind and judge him according to our beliefs? Who's to say what's right and wrong? So we better worry about our own problems and let the other guy worry about his.

I'm no judge. I don't want anybody judging me.

Some people didn't respect Ali because they say he talked too much. Yes, he talked a lot. I think it's safe to say that's one man who talked even more than I do. But didn't he back up every single word?

It's one thing to run off at the mouth about all the wonderful things you're going to do and then fail to produce. I've always said that the worst thing that ever could appear on your tombstone is "He had great potential." It's something totally different when you go out and finish exactly what you're yapping about.

Ali didn't just talk. He did it with style. He came up with all those fancy phrases—"float like a butterfly, sting like a bee." He wrote poems about himself. He told the world he was the greatest. Then he went out and proved it.

I remember when he fought Buster Mathis. Ali's theme for that fight was "I'm gonna do to Buster what the Indians did to Custer."

"He kept going around the country saying that all the time," Mathis said. "I thought I could beat him. But he kept on saying that and I started to wonder if he might not be telling the truth."

That's the way Ali was. His hands were so fast. His feet were so quick. Eventually time got to him. Nothing else could.

Ali was as quick with his mind as he was with his body. That's why I have so much respect for him.

Ali saved boxing. He made it into the multimillion-dollar sport it is today. Along the way, he made so many people happy. He was such a tremendous showman. What's wrong with that?

There are giants. Then there's Muhammad Ali.

I'm a sports junkie. There aren't too many sports I don't follow with a certain passion. I think the greatest invention since the double steal is ESPN. I watch everything.

My favorite is the NCAA college basketball tournament. For a month-long period, there isn't a greater spectacle in sports. Throughout the winter, I watch all the college games. I know all the teams from the East, the South, the Midwest, and the West. I know all the coaches and all the players. By the time the tournament comes and we're in spring training, I can pretty much tell the powerhouses and the sleepers.

During the season I watch as many baseball games as I can on TV. When I get home from a night game, I flip on one of the superstations and watch the National League. You'd be surprised how much you can scout other teams by following them on TV.

Just like every fan, I've got my favorites in every sport. But, to me, the true measure of any player's greatness is longevity. It doesn't matter what sport it is. If a player doesn't stick around for at least fifteen years he can't legitimately be called a superstar or a giant.

Walter Payton and Jimmy Brown are in a class by themselves in football. They were the finest runners ever to carry a ball. A coach could count on them every game. He knew they were going to give him at least one hundred yards. They carried the ball over and over and never got hurt. The other team knew they were getting the ball and still couldn't stop them. They were always ready for the next play . . . always ready for the next Sunday.

I appreciate that because it's like a workhorse pitcher in baseball. A pitcher might not be the biggest winner on a staff. But he might be the most valuable if he takes his turn every fifth day.

People don't realize how important that is to a manager. If I know I can count on a guy every fifth day, I can build my staff around him. I can set up the rest of my starters. I can pace my bullpen. Now I've got a plan.

If I've got a starter who might be in there one time and then miss a start here and another one there, I've got trouble. That one guy can throw off my whole staff.

That's the reliability Payton and Brown gave their coaches. They knew they could be counted on. They might have an off-game here and there. But everybody knew they'd be in the lineup. At least you could start with a game plan and see if it worked.

There were so many great quarterbacks in the NFL: Johnny Unitas, Fran Tarkenton, Joe Namath. They all stuck around for a long time. My all-time favorite is Roger Staubach. The reason is simple. Every time Dallas needed a big play, Staubach delivered.

I watched the Cowboys in all their glory years. It seemed like every time they needed a long drive late in the game, Staubach came up with one. He could march his club down the field quicker and better than anyone I've seen. he didn't play the clock, he played with it.

I love basketball. I only played a couple of years in high school and I probably was too short even for that. But I loved scrapping for the ball and shooting from the outside.

I followed the Lakers. Elgin Baylor was the first dominant player that I saw. He dominated the game. He did things back then that no other player could do. Nowadays it seems like everybody does them. Baylor was the forerunner to players like Magic Johnson and Michael Jordan.

We were at my mother's house once watching a Lakers game on TV. Baylor was in his prime. When he played, he had a little twitch in his neck.

I said to my mother, "Mom, do me a favor. Sit down and tell me who the best player is."

She didn't know diddly about basketball. After about five minutes she said, "How am I supposed to know? But that guy out there bobbing his head all the time looks like he's playing with kids."

That's how dominant Baylor was. You didn't need to know basketball to recognize his talent.

There are a lot of great players today. My top three are Magic Johnson, Michael Jordan, and Larry Bird. They can actually control a game. Those three guys are a show by themselves.

I would always pay to see Magic Johnson play. I would always pay to see Michael Jordan do all his slam dunks. I would always pay to see Larry Bird throw in baskets from the parking lot. I don't care who wins the game. I can watch those guys all night long.

I love playing golf. It's the one thing in life I've found that gives me peace and takes my mind off baseball. During the season I don't get the opportunity to play very often. During the off-season, I'm on the course every day it doesn't rain. When it rains I'm at the clubhouse waiting for it to stop. I'm not good, but I enjoy it.

I've always followed the pros. They're so much better and stronger now that it's almost a different game. The equipment is so improved and the pros hit the ball so much farther.

My two favorites remain Jack Nicklaus and Arnold Palmer.

Palmer was the first giant. Fans adored him. "Arnie's Army" is actually what helped turn golf into a spectator's game as well as a participant game. He had that vicious swing—the kind every once-a-week hacker has. But Arnie knew what to do with it. He had so much charm, so much charisma. He knew how to win with the chips down.

Then along came Nicklaus. He rewrote all the books Arnie had just written. Nothing scared him. It seemed like he could will a ball into the hole.

Golf's a lot like boxing. You're out there by yourself. You can't look for help. That's why I admire these guys so much.

Today there are so many good players. There always seems to be a new youngster running off a hot streak for a couple of years.

Nicklaus and Palmer did it for twenty years. They took on all challengers. They withstood the test of time. Galleries followed them regardless where they stood in a tournament. Their entourages were enormous.

I probably pay more attention to coaches than most fans do. There's no one I respect more than the coach who builds a winning program within all the rules and then is able to keep it going year after year. These are the real giants because they are responsible for the performance and actions of our finest athletes at the professional and college levels.

Bo Schembechler at the University of Michigan has got to be the finest football coach in the country. Every year his team finished in the top ten. It's a lock. He was there twenty years and not once was there the hint of a scandal with his players.

Lou Holtz is special. Every place that man has coached has become a winner. More importantly, he's made men out of boys. When he was at Arkansas he sat three of his stars out of the Orange Bowl against Oklahoma because they broke the rules. He did the same thing at Notre Dame when they played for the national championship against West Virginia in the Fiesta Bowl. That took guts. It taught a lesson in life to every young man on those teams.

I hold that same respect for Dean Smith at the University of North Carolina and Bobby Knight at Indiana. They do it year after year. John Wooden was the same way at UCLA before he retired. He not only developed great basketball players, he helped to mold men.

I think it's good to have heroes. But we must choose them with a lot of care. A hero must not only be able to do it on the field, he has to be a real human being. He has to show he cares.

Heroes stand for hope for all of us. They represent our dreams. That's a giant-sized burden. The giants do it with grace.

All of the giants—whether they be players, coaches, entertainers, politicians, or businessmen—are individuals on the outside. On the inside, though, I've got a feeling they're an awful lot the same. They share a tremendous sense of pride. They perform to the best of their ability regardless of the situation. Win or lose, these guys perform.

Parks

I played one year in the big leagues and drew the prize—
Philadelphia. They call it "The City of Brotherly Love," and
it's a great city. But if you ain't hitting, brother, don't expect hugs
and kisses.

There was a guy who had season tickets behind the Phillie
dugout. He showed up for every game with a bullhorn. When a
player who was struggling came up, he really gave him an earful.

That was only half the problem. His brother had season tickets
behind the visitors' dugout. After a while he came up with a
bullhorn, too. Now it's one thing to get an earful from one
section. But when you're scuffling, it's downright embarrassing
to get it in stereo.

I'd take one step out of the on deck circle and it sounded like a Don Rickles show. I'm glad my mother wasn't there. They knew my name was Anderson. But the names they used in front of it sure weren't Sparky.

Those were great times. I wouldn't trade that one year in the big leagues for anything in the world. I learned in a hurry that fans who pay big league ticket prices expect big league performances. And they have every right to do so.

Don't think fans can't affect a player's performance. If fans take a player in as their boy, generally that player responds to them. He knows they love him. For some reason, better things come out of him. If fans take off after a player, most of the time that young man dies.

Only the great ones rise above all that. Mike Schmidt did it in Philadelphia. He's one of the all-time great third basemen. He finished with 548 home runs. And those fans chewed him up and spit him out for a long time.

Schmidt was strong, though. He survived.

Fans sometimes affect how a manager manages. The good manager is sure of himself. He makes the moves he knows are right and doesn't worry about what other people think. But the shaky guys sometimes let the fans dictate their moves. They're weak and get run out of the game in a couple of years.

Billy Martin is a great example of one man who refused to run scared. Managing anywhere in the big leagues is like putting your brain in a pressure pot and turning the jets on high. Managing in New York takes that even further.

Billy was generally a fan favorite, but he had his share of second-guessers. Every manager does. In New York, those second-guessers have some mighty powerful lungs.

Don't think for a minute Billy ever made a move just to appease the fans. He had a plan and stuck to it. He was never afraid of what the fans might do . . . or anybody for that matter. Billy never ran scared.

Whitey Herzog is the same way in St. Louis. The Cardinals

draw close to 3 million every year. Baseball is a passion in St. Louis and the fans are as much a part of it as the players.

Whitey has to make some moves that the fans might not fully understand or appreciate, but that doesn't change his mind. That's one of the reasons he's been so successful wherever he's been.

Different parks force a manager to manage differently. If you're playing in Houston or St. Louis, for instance, you play to steal one run here and another one there. But at Minnesota, Detroit, Philadelphia, Wrigley, Atlanta, and Boston, let your hitters loose. You better score some runs because the other guys are going to light up the board.

It doesn't always work. But a team tailors itself to the park it plays in.

I've been fortunate to manage in every major league park. I enjoy the special features of each one. I love all the nooks and crannies . . . all the different colors and smells. I love to study the fans. I don't even have to see the field to know what city I'm in. I can tell just by watching the fans.

The two best hitters' parks are Minnesota and Philadelphia. The two best for pitchers are Houston and St. Louis.

I like almost all the parks for different reasons. My five runaway favorites are: Dodger Stadium, Anaheim, Kansas City, Cincinnati, and Detroit, but it's fun to visit all of them.

NATIONAL LEAGUE

ATLANTA—ATLANTA–FULTON COUNTY STADIUM

Just on looks, the park is very ordinary. There are no special features at all. For hitters, though, it's the closest thing we have to Cape Kennedy. It's a rocket range. If you can hit the ball up in the air often enough, you'll get your share of homers. When I managed in the National League, the infield was alive, too. You could skip balls all over the place.

My teams always had success there because we were so strong. We'd just stand up at the plate and whack away. If I was a big, strong hitter, I'd get down on my knees and beg to get traded to Atlanta.

One of the weirdest and scariest things I ever saw in baseball happened when we were playing at Atlanta.

It was so hot I don't know how any of the players made it through the day. It seemed like 100 degrees with 100 percent humidity. You broke a sweat as soon as you walked out of the clubhouse. Of all the times, we had to go extra innings.

In the top of the tenth inning, Lee May broke the tie by hitting a home run for us. Of course, we were happy to take the lead, but we also were happy that it looked like we would finally get out of that place.

May was trotting around the bases. When he got to third, it looked like he completely ran out of gas. He had all he could do to force himself home. I remember some of the guys in the dugout joking and yelling out, "Come on, big boy, you can make it."

He did . . . just barely. All of a sudden, it didn't seem so funny.

When he finally touched the plate, he couldn't go any more. He flat out could not take another step. He was totally dehydrated. He didn't pass out, but he could not move another inch. His whole body cramped up.

Our trainer came and we helped him to the clubhouse. May was like a board. Our trainer filled a tub with ice and we had to put May in there so he could loosen up.

CHICAGO—WRIGLEY FIELD

Look out! If the wind's blowing out, nobody's safe. Not even the people across the street.

Wrigley Field is tradition. When you walk out on that field, you know you're supposed to play a ball game. Of course, when I was there, there weren't any lights. I remember a lot of afternoons when it got late and we had to hurry to get the game in.

I appreciate tradition. But I can't fault them for putting in lights. That's the way the game is played today.

Cub fans are characters. It seems like all their fans walked out of a Damon Runyan book. They're loud, but they're good fans.

I remember the year I played for Philadelphia. They talked to me when I was in the on-deck circle.

"Anderson, why do you even waste your time going up there?" they'd yell.

Finally I turned around and told them; "You guys are probably right. But the rules say I've got to take my hacks. If I could go back to that dugout right now, I'd be happier than you having to watch me try to hit."

After that, they cheered for me all the time.

CINCINNATI—RIVERFRONT STADIUM

There ain't no place like it. When you talk about down-to-earth, middle-of-the-gut Midwestern America, you're talking about Cincinnati. There's a smack of South to it. Kentucky is right across the river. Overall though, it's Midwest all the way. Very conservative. Very friendly.

The fans expect so much because they're so used to winning. They're spoiled. But they're good fans. They're loyal. They're just like Tiger, Cub, or Cardinal fans. Once you become a fan for one of those teams, you're hooked for life.

When you manage there, everybody knows you. People walk up to you on the street. If you're driving a car, they might tap on your window at a stoplight. They don't bother you. They're just friendly.

Riverfront Stadium is magnificent. You'll never be in a stadium that's better run. Even with 52,000 people, thirty minutes after a game, the place is empty and the area is clear. There's no congestion. From the clubhouses to the concession stands, the working conditions are fantastic.

The only thing I don't like about Riverfront Stadium is the Astroturf. Playing baseball on Astroturf is like playing basketball on an ice rink. It's not the same game.

Outfielders have to play deeper so the balls in the alleys don't skip by. Infielders also have to play deeper or they'll get killed from the hops. Once a ball hits on that stuff, it picks up speed. If a ball is hit to the side of an infielder, generally it gets through.

The seams where the artificial surface is sewn together are deadly. We lost a game in the 1972 World Series when a routine ground ball to third hit a seam and bounced over Dennis Menke's head for a hit. This happened in Cincinnati but it could have happened anywhere there's artificial turf. In my career, I've seen at least twenty-five balls hit a seam and bounce over a fielder's head or past him in some crazy way.

HOUSTON—ASTRODOME

I never liked the Dome. It's too big and the atmosphere is definitely not baseball. When I managed there I always felt like I was in a stage show. The seats are like those in a theater. I always felt like they had glass on top of the dugout and people were staring at me.

It's the toughest park I've ever seen to hit a home run out of. King Kong would have to crank it to get it out of there. Glenn Davis really shows me something. Hitting thirty homers a year playing half his games there, he must be a superman.

I saw so many balls absolutely crushed that got out to the warning track and then died. They dropped straight down like a dead duck.

If I were a pitcher, I'd fight to get to Houston. If Jack Morris had pitched his whole career in Houston, he would have had more than two hundred wins already.

LOS ANGELES—DODGER STADIUM

There'll never be another ballpark with a setting as beautiful as Dodger Stadium. I don't care how old that stadium ever gets to be, there'll never be another one that stays as clean and new as that one. This is baseball's Disneyland. It's immaculate every single day of the year.

It's a fair park. It's a good park to hit in and a good one to pitch in. That makes players want to play.

Dodger fans are great fans. They love baseball. But going to a Dodger game is like going to a show. It's entertainment. It's the place to be and be seen.

They leave in the sixth or seventh inning sometimes. It's not because they don't love the game. What they really want to do is beat the traffic. Traffic is murder all over Los Angeles. Getting out of the ballpark is suicidal. People jump into their cars and immediately switch on the game on the radio. They want to know what happened. But they don't want to sit in traffic all night.

They are not hard fans. They are very soft fans. A player can do a lot of things wrong there and the fans won't bother him. If a player screws up in some cities, he might get garbage dumped on his head. Dodger fans don't crucify a player because he didn't get a hit.

I loved managing there because I was so close to home. I didn't get a thrill because of all the celebrities that go there. But I did enjoy being in that park. I'd pay just to go sit in the bleachers.

MONTREAL—OLYMPIC STADIUM

The park they play in now is beautiful. I go way back to the old park where I managed in AAA. You can't imagine a worse place. If anyone thought the old Toronto park was bad, then they never saw the one in Montreal.

I understand the Montreal fan is catching on to the game a

little more now. When I was there, they really didn't understand baseball. They didn't have a chance to get really critical.

When I was there, Montreal fans just showed up to see the game. It didn't matter who won. They just wanted to see baseball.

NEW YORK—SHEA STADIUM

Shea is a fair park for a player. If a batter connects, the ball goes out. If a pitcher is sharp, he throws a good game. He ain't cheated by the park. I remember the infield being hard and balls bouncing through like a tennis court. But overall, the park is fair.

Still, I just don't like it. It's not a great stadium as far as I'm concerned. It seems like there's always chaos, just like there's chaos in New York.

I love visiting New York for three days. I truly enjoy those three days. I walk around in amazement at all the buildings and the shows and the restaurants. I can't believe there are so many people. After three days, though, I'm ready to leave. There's no way I can take any more. It's not me.

Fans in New York know baseball as well as any fans in the country. They were raised on baseball. They understand the game. They are tremendous fans. But New York fans are hard fans. They are a reflection of the city. They're just like it. They have to be tough. You ain't gonna survive there unless you are tough. And there are a lot of survivors.

PHILADELPHIA—VETERANS STADIUM

A true hitters' park. I don't know why, but the ball pops there. If you take a team into Philadelphia, you better put some runs on the scoreboard.

This is a tough atmosphere. I know why Rocky Balboa had to come from Philadelphia. Philly fans are some of the greatest in the country. They love sports. All sports. They're tough because they understand the games so well.

226

There's nothing greater than being a professional athlete in Philadelphia . . . as long as you produce. If you produce, you are an idol. But only for that moment.

The writers there have razors in their typewriters. They go for the jugular. They skip right over everything else. They miss no one, either. Schmidt was one of the greatest players in history. Steve Carlton was one of the greatest pitchers. They chopped them up and spit them out like they were eating lunch.

Nobody gets a free ride in Philly. It's a great place to play, but you better have lizard skin.

PITTSBURGH—THREE RIVERS STADIUM

Three Rivers is nice, but it's not one of my favorite stadiums. It looks too much like so many others.

Whenever I go there I always think about all those monster shots Willie Stargell hit. I look way up into the upper deck and can't believe he actually hit baseballs that far.

The Pittsburgh game I remember more than any other took place in 1971. Dock Ellis hit the first three batters he faced in the first inning—Pete Rose, Ken Griffey, and Joe Morgan. I never saw anything like it.

The Pittsburgh Steelers were the big cats in town back then. It seemed like they were always going to the Super Bowl. They used to practice there and I remember talking a lot to Coach Chuck Noll and owner Art Rooney. I always liked to find out how a professional football coach handled his players.

ST. LOUIS—BUSCH STADIUM

St. Louis is the Midwest and I love it. People there are so friendly and are true baseball fans. The Cardinals enjoy that rich tradition. Fans there are loyal. They live and die with the Cardinals, but they aren't vicious to opposing teams. No matter who makes the play, they cheer a good one. They don't verbally abuse you the way it is in some cities.

Bob Gibson had really passed his prime when I used to visit St. Louis. But when we came in, he seemed to reach back for a little extra. I remember a game when he struck out thirteen of our batters. We got two hits off him and both were flares.

Joe Torre showed me a lot by winning a batting title there. It's hard to hit home runs there so he became a line-drive hitter. He learned to use the middle and not try to do what can't be done.

St. Louis builds a team with speed and pitching. They get players like Vince Coleman, Willie McGee, Gary Templeton, Jose Oquendo. They bounce and run and use the whole field.

SAN DIEGO—JACK MURPHY STADIUM

The first thing that impresses you about San Diego is the weather. It just might be the finest all-around climate in the country. You never feel cold at the park. The nights are just a hair cool so you don't feel heat or moisture. That's ideal for a player.

It helps to create a very competitive atmosphere. A player should be able to perform here. There's no excuse not to.

When I was in the National League, the fans didn't get overly excited about the Padres or anything that happened on the field. They were an expansion club and that's basically how the fans treated them. The Chargers were number 1.

Now it's changed. When we played the Padres in the 1984 World Series, I couldn't believe I was in the same park I used to go to.

In Game One, the fans were so loud I never thought any crowd could top it. They did, though, in Game Two. There was no rowdiness, just a lot of noise and a lot of excitement.

SAN FRANCISCO—CANDLESTICK PARK

For me, they could file that place forever. It's the coldest, most awful place I've ever been to. It doesn't matter if it's April or August, it's still the same. At night, it's freezing cold.

We used to have hibachis going in the dugout every night just to try to keep warm. There was nothing you could do about the wind. I swear one night I saw a ball hit deep to right center field. The wind took it all the way to the foul pole and it barely wrapped around it.

I've seen some great hitters play there. Those guys deserve a lot of credit. How anybody can ever hit there for a career is way beyond me. Guys like Will Clark and Kevin Mitchell are not only outstanding hitters, but they have tremendous constitutions. They are able to shut out all the conditions and excel. They've got great mental toughness, the sign of true pros.

AMERICAN LEAGUE

BALTIMORE—MEMORIAL STADIUM

There's a lot of American history attached to Baltimore. Whenever I go there, I immediately think of two people—Babe Ruth and Al Kaline.

This is the home of The Babe. I always try to picture what he looked like as a kid. I wonder what sandlots he played on. I wonder if he was a bully growing up or if he cared about playing sports at all.

Kaline is one of our television announcers. I never saw him in his prime except for spring training and All-Star Games. To go into the Hall of Fame on the first ballot, though, he had to be special.

The Oriole organization impressed me by the way it turned itself around from 107 losses in 1988 to losing the pennant on the next to last day of the 1989 season. That is almost unbelievable. The park itself is old, but I don't mind it. It's nothing special, just a good place to play baseball.

BOSTON—FENWAY PARK

Fenway Park is one of the oldest parks in baseball. There's no rhyme or reason to its design. As for conveniences, there are none.

It's really not a baseball park. It's got weird angles in the outfield. You can't make heads or tails out of distances to the fences. Then there's that jolly green giant staring at you from left field. It's not a ballpark. It's a shooting gallery. You almost need a computer to keep track of all the ground rules.

But I love being there. Everybody does. There's an aura about that park. There is so much history in it. I swear ghosts live somewhere out in those bleachers or behind that left field wall. This is the place where Ted Williams was the man.

Boston fans are remarkable. They love baseball. They understand the game and die with the Red Sox. They're very tough fans. Very, very tough.

I've got a great relationship with them because they appreciate the game so much.

I never had more fun in the opposing city of the World Series than I did in Boston in 1975.

CALIFORNIA—ANAHEIM STADIUM

Dodger Stadium is number 1, Royals Stadium is number 2, and Anaheim is number 3. You could throw those three names up in the air. Whichever one came down first, I'd be happy with.

Anaheim is gorgeous. The playing facilities are great. The parking is great for the fans. The landscaping is beautiful. It was even prettier before they added all those seats in the outfield. But the conditions in Anaheim are ideal. A player has no excuse for not performing well there.

As much as I love the park, it was the site of one of the worst games in my career. In 1986 we took a 12–5 lead into the last of the ninth. We got two outs before they made it 12–7. When it was over, Dick Schofield hit a grand slam off Willie Hernandez to win it 13–12.

That's the most runs a team has scored in the ninth inning to win a game. It taught me one very important lesson that I carry today—no lead is ever safe until it's over. Yogi Berra was 100 percent right.

Angel fans are a little tougher than Dodger fans. But not much. Basically, they're at the park to have fun. It's a night out and the place to be. They don't get on the visiting manager like they do in some other cities.

We get a lot of Tiger fans at the park when we play there because so many people have moved to Southern California from other areas, including Detroit.

CHICAGO—COMISKEY PARK

Just going to Chicago makes me happy because it's my favorite city to walk. There's always a lot of excitement in Chicago.

There's a lot of history in Comiskey because it's an old park. The fans there are different from the ones at Wrigley Field. Cubbie fans show up all summer, regardless of how the team is doing. All they want to do is be Cubs fans. White Sox fans are a little tougher. When they get hold of a player, they like to grind him into the ground. On the south side of town, the boys better be winning.

I remember one game, though, where the fans were pulling for us. Actually, for Jack Morris. It was a Saturday afternoon in April 1984 and we were the Game of the Week. Jack fired a no-hitter and finished the game by striking out Ron Kittle with a forkball that dropped off the face of the earth. I always think of that game when I visit Comiskey.

CLEVELAND—CLEVELAND STADIUM

I wish I could have seen Cleveland Stadium back in the forties and fifties when the Indians put those great pitching staffs together. They had guys like Bob Feller, Early Wynn, Bob Lemon, and Mike Garcia. That must have been something when they filled the place. They won 111 games in 1954. The place had to be rocking.

When we go there now, it seems like there's 8,000 to 10,000 people. I feel like I'm walking through a morgue. The place is too big for baseball. Even if you draw 50,000, there are still 30,000 empty seats.

It's tough for me to play there because there never seems to be any action going on. It's like they invited two teams to show up in this monster stadium and no one knew about it. Something seems to be missing. It's just too big.

DETROIT—TIGER STADIUM

Here's how to approach Tiger Stadium. Drive south on the Lodge Freeway and get off on Trumbull. As soon as you get off the ramp—smack, it hits you.

There's nothing like it. This is what a baseball stadium is supposed to be like. The light towers grab you. They stand proud like flags to let you know this is a major league baseball stadium. This is what the artist had in mind when he painted a ballpark.

I don't care if this does sound corny. Whenever I see it, I still get a thrill. Sometimes I say to myself, "And I'm the manager here?"

I've made history managing in Detroit ten years. This is the same place where Ty Cobb and Charlie Gehringer and Hank Greenberg and Al Kaline and so many stars played.

It's the same stadium. The same field. Even the uniforms have stayed the same. Nothing has changed. It's as if time has stopped. Except for the Yankees, I don't believe there's another team with more tradition or has a greater aura than the Tigers. And they're not far behind.

Part of that credit belongs to their fans. Detroit people are unbelievable sports fans. Not just for baseball, but for any sport. You could throw a shoe up in the air, call it a new game and they'd pack the joint to see it.

Michigan people are tough fans. But they're a good tough. These are all hardworking people. Many of them are blue collar. They work in the auto factory all day. They earn their money. And when they spend it, they expect an honest effort in return.

There's nothing wrong with that. They treat you the way you treat them. I tell that to every player that comes to Detroit. If you bust your tail every game and don't do well, they'll never bother you. But short-change them and they'll nail you.

They know when a player is busting his butt. All they ever ask in Detroit is for the best effort you've got. You can't fool them, because they know sports.

There ain't a city in America like Detroit when it comes to sports. If you want proof, just look at how many athletes live there after their careers are over compared to other cities. It ain't for the weather. It's because they're treated like kings.

KANSAS CITY—ROYALS STADIUM

Except for the artificial grass, this is the ideal baseball park. That covers everything—beauty, field facilities, parking, press box, eating facilities. You name it, that park has it.

Other than the Tigers, I don't think you'll find an organization that's run better than the Royals. It is high class.

Fans there are fantastic. It's Midwest. A workingman's area all the way. People are low-key, friendly, and show you a lot of warmth when you visit. I liken Royals fans to those in Milwaukee and Cincinnati. They're loyal Royal all the way. But they're not tough fans. They're gracious. They receive and treat the visiting team very well. A player doesn't have to worry about being insulted there.

The only thing I'd like to change is to have the stadium hold an extra 10,000. I think they could handle it.

MILWAUKEE—MILWAUKEE COUNTY STADIUM

I know why "Happy Days" was set in Milwaukee.

There's not much to do there, but I love every visit. This is the heartland. These are regular people. No Hollywood or Tinseltown in them. They're straight up. When they talk, you better listen.

Milwaukee is just like Kansas City without Royals Stadium. The Milwaukee park is all right, but it's getting old. I'd love to see them get a new one because I know that city could handle it.

It's a good hitters' park. All the fences are reachable. I remember all too well a 1985 game that ended with a grand slam Ted Simmons cranked off Willie Hernandez in the ninth.

Great fans. They're not wishy-washy. They don't get up on their players one day and down the next. They stick with them. It's a great place for players to play.

MINNESOTA—HUBERT H. HUMPHREY METRODOME

I love the city. I don't like the park.

I don't like the park because it's not meant for baseball. There are too many things that happen in there that really aren't part of the game. Balls bounce around like you're playing pool. Line drives become guided missiles. Fielders have to play back when they should be in and come in when they should be back.

I saw one of the craziest plays ever there and all because of Astroturf. Lou Whitaker hit a blooper down the left field line late in the game. The left fielder, the third baseman, and the short-stop all chased it. It landed between them and wound up rolling all the way to the left field corner. Meanwhile Lou kept chugging around the bases and ended up with a game-winning inside-the-park home run.

You'd better be able to put runs on the board because the Twins are going to slap you with a trainful. That's the way they build their team. They're bruisers.

I would have never believed they'd ever draw 3 million people there. But now the Twins are number 1. They're the kings of Minnesota.

NEW YORK—YANKEE STADIUM

It won't matter how many awards I win or how many times I go there, I'll always get chills when I walk into Yankee Stadium. They can remodel the place all they want. History will live there forever.

Casey Stengel defined managing there. Babe Ruth played there; so did Lou Gehrig, Joe DiMaggio, Mickey Mantle, Yogi Berra ... the list goes on and on. All those World Series. All those great plays.

It's a very tough place for visiting teams to play. Not only do you have to beat the Yankees, you have to battle all those ghosts. Believe me, the ghosts are for real.

I love watching a young player walk into Yankee Stadium for the first time. He tries not to show it, but his heart starts to pound like a drum. I know. Mine still does.

Yankee fans know baseball, and they can be vicious. A player must prepare himself for that before he walks into the stadium.

If you don't pull the ball, you've really got to drill it there. Those gaps eat hitters alive.

Yankee Stadium is a shrine.

OAKLAND—OAKLAND COLISEUM

It's a great place to play an honest-to-goodness baseball game. That's because there's not a trick in the park. If you do it, you deserve it. If you don't, it's not the park's fault.

They have a great infield. Outfield fences are reachable, but they're not Christmas gifts. You must connect, but you won't be cheated. There's a lot of room from the foul lines to the stands so a fielder has a chance on every ball.

Oakland is just across the bay from San Francisco, but the weather is so different. It's always pleasant and good for a game.

The fans are very hard. They get with the action and get on the visiting team something fierce. That's a little of the West Coast element. They're a lot like San Francisco fans. There is a difference, though. At San Francisco you also have to fight the weather. In Oakland, all you have to fight are the fans.

SEATTLE—THE KINGDOME

I can't get a line on Seattle. It's a beautiful part of the country. I love to walk all those hills and look at the waterfront and all the greenery. The ballpark, though, is awful. I walk in there and I'm not sure what I'm in. It's just a big ball of cement. There's no color, no nothing. It seems like a big factory.

We've never had good luck in Seattle and there was one series there I'll never forget. We had just swept three straight from the Angels in Anaheim in 1984 to run our record to 35–5. We were hotter than a shipload of sailors on a Saturday night.

Until we got to Seattle, that is.

236

The Mariners swept us three straight games. We couldn't do a thing right and they couldn't do a thing wrong. I remember all the brooms the fans brought to the park on the last day to give us a sweep.

I don't know if the people are baseball fans or not. They haven't shown up through the turnstiles. I know they're great football and basketball fans, but I haven't seen any big crowds at the baseball games yet.

TEXAS—ARLINGTON STADIUM

I love Texas for the simple reason we go right out the hotel door and walk across the parking lot to the park. I wouldn't know downtown Dallas if somebody dropped me into the middle of it.

I go for a walk there at nine A.M. By eleven-thirty I'm back at the hotel. At noon I'm at the park. The manager's office there is big and I usually catch up on a lot of work.

I believe they need a new stadium. It gets so hot in the summer. The heat definitely wears down a player come July and August. This is one place where they should have a dome.

This is actually a different park since they added some outfield walls a few years ago. It used to be King Kong couldn't hit a homer to right because of the winds. Now with the walls, balls fly out of there. I'll always remember a two-run homer right down the right field line by Kirk Gibson off Charlie Hough in the ninth inning to win a game in 1987.

TORONTO—THE SKYDOME

The Skydome is quite a spectacle. It proves what great planning, great engineering, and great imagination can do. Once they refine all of it, they'll draw 3.5 to 4 million people a year because it's a showplace.

It will become a tourist attraction. Everyone who goes to Toronto will want to see the Skydome. It will be like Disneyland. They've not only built a great stadium, they've built an attraction. I don't like any stadium that has a dome or artificial turf. But I can't help but like the Skydome.

I'm the only manager ever to manage in all three Toronto parks, going back to my minor league days. We used to draw over 500,000 fans a season. That's a lot for the minor leagues, especially back then. Once fans started to watch the big league games on TV, the attendance started to decline. Time started to run out on the minor leagues.

I've seen the fans change over the years. They've come to understand baseball. They used to be goody-goody fans. All they wanted to do was see their Blue Jays—win or lose.

Now they've become harsher. Now they want to win. They no longer accept losing. They're very courteous fans, very polite—but they want to win.

Thank You

Twenty years is a long time for anything. For managing in the big leagues, it's almost an eternity.

I leafed through the record book to check how many men in major league history have managed at least twenty years. I knew there haven't been many. I was surprised to discover though, that I now am only the fourteenth.

I can't believe twenty years have come and gone already. It seems like I can remember every game just as if it had been played last week. I remember all the players, all the umpires, all the writers. I even recall some of the faces in the stands.

I've been very lucky. Three times my teams have won World

Championships. Of those thirteen other guys with twenty years, some weren't fortunate enough to have won one.

So choosing my most gratifying year should be pretty easy. The choices are obvious: 1975—my first World Championship after one of the most dramatic World Series in history; 1976—my second straight championship with one of the greatest teams in baseball history; 1984—a World Championship with the Detroit Tigers making me the first manager in history to win a World Series in both leagues.

I treasure all three of those years and all those memories. They're very precious, very special.

The most gratifying year of my career, though, is 1989.

That's the year my team was hammered for 103 losses. That's the year my team finished last, light years out of first place. That's the year I had to return home in the middle of the season to get my head straight.

It's also the year I became a more complete human being. It was the year I realized Sparky Anderson isn't the specially blessed person I thought he was. It was the year George Anderson became more in touch with himself and the reality of life than he had been his first fifty-five years on this planet.

I don't want any Tiger fans to think for a minute that I wanted our team to lose 103 games. I'd be the first one to tell everybody that I wish this wouldn't have happened.

But it did. Like Casey once said, "It's in the book. You can look it up."

From the pain, though, I was blessed with a sobering realization. Losing the way we did and undergoing the turmoil I did provided a certain insight that isn't available to the person who hasn't had to suffer. Yet 1989 helped to give me an understanding, not only of my own life, but of all the people in the world who have to survive daily with suffering other people can't even imagine.

I'm not a psychologist so I can't explain the mental mechanics. And I won't insult anyone by equating losses on a baseball field to the suffering that some people must endure every day of their lives. All I know is that I have a completely different viewpoint when it comes to suffering. I see it almost from another dimension. I can feel it. I never came close to understanding that feeling until my ordeal of 1989.

A couple of years ago, I started a charitable foundation in Detroit called CATCH. It stands for Caring Athletes' Team for Children's and Henry Ford Hospitals. We generate money to help underprivileged kids who don't have the chance to experience life the way most kids do.

The foundation is something new, but I had always been involved with visiting kids at hospitals even back in my days at Cincinnati. I had a deal with Children's Hospital in Cincinnati. As long as they never advertised that I was coming, I visited the kids once each home stand. I brought players along with me after I had fined them for something.

Their fine was to throw some kind of party for the kids. One week it would be an ice cream party. The next would be a pizza party. Then maybe a McDonald's party.

I did that my whole nine years at Cincinnati. The nurses were great. When I got fired, they all got together and released this story to the press.

I have to admit I was grateful to them. I was grateful that they had kept it secret for nine years. Then I was thankful they released it because it made me feel good to know they cared about my visits.

I've got a similar deal in Detroit where I visit Children's and Henry Ford Hospitals. I throw pizza parties. Our owner, Tom Monaghan, also owns Domino's Pizza, and he's quite generous supplying pizza for the kids.

I'm not breaking any secret because when I was sent home during the 1989 season, the nurses in Detroit told the press. All the kids, doctors, and nurses at the hospitals sent a giant get well card to me while I was recuperating at home. I was really touched.

I've been doing these visits now for twenty years. But I really never knew exactly what was going on. When I walked away from the hospital each week, I felt I had done a little bit of good. I watched the kids' faces when I walked into the room. Some of them were too sick to understand what was going on, but a lot of them recognized me and their eyes would open like saucers. It made them feel good that someone would take the time to show them he cared.

I felt I had contributed something. But I felt good mainly because my children and my grandchildren weren't suffering as these kids were. My kids didn't have the problems these kids had.

The youngsters are the ones who really suffer. That suffering, though, touches so many other people: the fathers, the mothers, the sisters, the brothers, the grandfathers, the grandmothers, all of those youngsters' friends.

When I go to the hospitals now I look at all these people. I don't have to look too long. That pain is written all over their faces. They can't hide it. It shows like a flashing neon sign.

I remember one particular case last summer at Henry Ford Hospital. There was a precious five-year-old girl who came within an eyelash of dying. Even the doctors were surprised she survived. One of the doctors told me that this child's mother came dangerously close to breaking herself. Somehow by the grace of God, this little girl rallied. I remember going there the next week. When I walked into the room the mother was holding her child. The child still had tubes all over her body, but she was on her way back.

The little girl's grandma was sitting next to her. Grandpa was standing by the door. When I walked in, I joked with Grandpa.

"I see you're the guard today," I said.

He smiled and nodded with a $100 gleam in his eye.

"Yes sir, I'm the guard," he said.

They were all so happy. All so proud. Nothing in the world could have bothered them.

Sometimes we don't realize how far-reaching the illness of one child is. It touches so many people. The depression is almost like a plague.

Now I'm not about to suggest in any way that just because I went through a horrible losing season I can appreciate all the real suffering that exists in this world. Not for a minute. But for whatever reason, I am now truly able to understand one-tenth of one percent of what these mothers and fathers have to go through.

That's not much and I sure don't know why, but at least now I can appreciate it a lot more than I used to.

A baseball game is going to go away. A losing streak is going to go away. So is a bad season. What some of these kids must suffer doesn't go away. This monster stays. It sticks around simply to haunt the minds of the child, the mother, the father, all the family, and all the friends. They all go to bed each night praying that when they wake up, things will be different. But it doesn't work that way.

That's the beauty of baseball. No matter how bad you are, eventually it will go away. Even if the bad lasts for a whole season, every day you go to the park, you've got a chance to win.

The greatest example I've ever seen of this was the 1989 Baltimore Orioles. That team lost 107 games in 1988. They bounced back the very next year and came closer than wet on water to winning the whole thing.

They didn't go to spring training in 1989 starting out with 107 losses. No one told them they couldn't win because they had lost 107 games the year before. They all just rolled up their sleeves, went to work, and turned it all around.

The 1989 Tigers finished last. I never dreamed we would lose so many games. But come 1990, we get a fresh chance.

How much more can anyone ask for? At least we get the chance to start over. This is something I never really understood before. Now I do.

I spent my first nineteen years in the major leagues blaming myself for every loss. I put that suffering on myself. But I never had to go through a season where we lost consistently. Night after night after night. Years ago I remember saying to myself, "How can those guys feel losing ninety to a hundred games year after year?"

Well, I found out. It ain't pleasant. But you learn to live through it because you realize there's always another chance. Now I know how every one of those guys feel.

He feels horrible. He feels like he's suffering. He feels ashamed of himself. He feels embarrassed. He feels all these things.

I've taken it one step further. Yes, I want to win again. I'll work even harder to get back there. But now there's a difference.

Winning now is a wish for me. It's no longer an obsession. Losing is not a tragedy. Not getting the chance to win or lose is the tragedy.

For the first time in my life I finally understand what baseball really is. It's a game. It's a game you must play hard, but it's still a game.

You play baseball because you love it. You work in it because you enjoy it. It's not right to make it a misery or a drudgery. I made baseball a drudgery. That ain't what baseball expects you to make of it.

Every year there's going to be only one eventual winner. There are going to be three other partial winners. There are going to be about a dozen clubs who will be decent. And the rest of the clubs will have a bad year. The bottom line, though, is that every one of us will have the same chance once the new season starts. That goes from the World Series champion to the team that finished with the worst record.

For nineteen years I had all the fortunes in the world and never took the time to say thank you. All I ever thought was that's the way things were supposed to be. There are no "supposed to be's." We are not entitled to have everything go our way. I used to think that I was entitled to winning. Losing was for the other guy. Throughout all of those years I used to tell Carol, "I don't know why . . . but God has blessed me to be a winner."

God didn't bless me to be a winner any more than He blesses

Charlie or Frank or Pete or whoever. I was just lucky. And I took all that luck for granted.

Then one day I got a whipping. Not just a whipping. A good, old-fashioned butt kicking that lasted a whole season. When it first happened, I didn't realize it. Now I know it's the best thing that ever happened to me. It's helped me to understand just what kind of suffering some people must go through.

I have a better understanding now what people go through when they get beat all the time. I can better understand the people who struggle because they have no money. I can better understand the sick people and those around them who suffer because there is no tomorrow for them. I can touch all the different people now. Before I couldn't touch anyone but myself.

I saw one of the greatest things in sports in 1989. That was Jim Abbott pitching for the California Angels. In fact, I don't think there's a better example for kids or adults. And I don't mean for handicapped people. I think Jim Abbott is a better example for healthy people than anyone else.

Here's a young man who was born with one hand. Not only did he make it to the major leagues, but he also became a key to the Angel starting rotation.

Every newspaper, magazine, and TV station made a big deal out of Abbott having just one hand. Not once, though, did you ever hear Jim say a word about it. He shows healthy people that if you don't have the courage to compete then there's something wrong with you.

I don't mean just competing in sports. I mean competing in life.

Nobody likes to lose. Losing hurts. Don't let anyone tell you anything different. There's a difference, though, between losing and being a loser. Losing is something that happens to everyone. It's life. Even winners must take their share of losing.

Being a loser is altogether different. A loser allows himself to get beaten and then feels sorry for himself without trying to do anything about it. He wallows in his sorrow. He's blind to the fact that people who really suffer don't have time to feel sorry for themselves.

When I lose a game now, I still hurt. Don't think for a minute that every loss doesn't slice to the bone. But now I understand when to put a stop to that hurt. I refuse to let it take me over the edge. It took me nineteen years to learn that limit. That's a long time to wake up.

I hope that young people learn that lesson a lot quicker than I did. If they and their children are blessed with their health, they should wake up to it immediately and not waste a day.

I'll never cry over a baseball game again. Baseball is a passing thing. Once the game is over, there's always another game. Once the season's over, there's always another year.

That little boy with cancer doesn't get a chance like that. That little boy will stay in my mind long after my career is over. I'll always remember that child as someone who never had a chance to take his lumps. I had my ups and downs. I suffered some lumps. At least I had the chance. That's the greatest gift of all.

That's why even though 1989 was painful, it was a blessing. I had to go home to find that out. I had to get back into the real world to appreciate all the suffering that goes on around us. But 1989 was a blessing.

Losing opened my eyes. I'm not special. I deserve a whipping, too. Now I know how the other guys felt. I had the bullwhip before. I used to hand out that whipping. I didn't know how much it stung on the other end.

I've always been nice to people, but I'm not sure I ever took the time to really feel for them. I do now. I don't pass a man on the street that I don't have compassion for.

It's a strange twist, but 1989 is the best year that ever happened to me. It's the year I became a genuine person. Not a person just for the good times. But one who's there to help out during the bad.

Thank you.

The Record

The beauty of Sparky Anderson doesn't lie simply in all of his baseball records. His true beauty comes from the soul and the color of his character. Sparky is a genuinely good person. He also is a legitimate character whose wit and charm transcends all the records in the book.

Nevertheless, the numbers are impressive. In fact, they're more than impressive. They're downright overwhelming.

Sparky has reached the point in his career where every victory carries historical significance. Sparky has reached the level where his records now rank in the all-time categories. He is no longer just part of history; Sparky is making history.

Health permitting, Sparky will continue to inch to the top of all the major managerial categories. He currently is the dean of American League managers, having been named manager of the Tigers on June 12, 1979. With 237 more victories, Sparky will become the all-time winningest manager in Tiger history. Hughie Jennings, from 1907 through 1920, set the record of 1,131.

Sparky is already the all-time Cincinnati leader with 863.

With his outstanding records, Sparky is the only manager in history to have won at least 800 games with two different teams.

Sparky enjoys a couple of other exclusives. He is the only manager in history to win a World Series in both leagues and the only one to win 100 or more games in a season with two different teams.

Sparky also has been named Manager of the Year in both leagues and is the only manager in history to guide two different teams to League Championship Series sweeps.

Those are the numbers. And with Sparky being just fifty-six years young, they're obviously still going up.

Baseball's 10 Winningest Managers

		W	L	Pct.
1	Connie Mack	3776	4025	.484
2	John McGraw	2840	1984	.589
3	Bucky Harris	2159	2219	.493
4	Joe McCarthy	2126	1335	.614
5	Walter Alston	2040	1613	.558
6	Leo Durocher	2010	1710	.540
7	Casey Stengel	1926	1867	.508
8	Gene Mauch	1901	2037	.483
9	Bill McKechnie	1898	1724	.524
10	**Sparky Anderson**	1758	1363	.563

Baseball's Best Percentages

20th Century and at least 10 years experience

		W	L	Pct.
1	Joe McCarthy	2126	1335	.614
2	Fred Clarke	1422	969	.595
3	Billy Southworth	1064	729	.593
4	Frank Chance	932	640	.593
5	John McGraw	2840	1984	.589
6	Earl Weaver	1480	1060	.583
7	Al Lopez	1422	1026	.581
8	**Sparky Anderson**	1758	1363	.563

Most World Series Games Managed

1	Casey Stengel	63
2	John McGraw	54
3	Connie Mack	43
4	Joe McCarthy	43
5	Walter Alston	40
6	Miller Huggins	33
7	**Sparky Anderson**	28

Most World Series Games Won

1	Casey Stengel	37
2	Joe McCarthy	30
3	John McGraw	26
4	Connie Mack	24
5	Walter Alston	20
6	Miller Huggins	18
7	**Sparky Anderson**	16

Most LCS Games Managed

1	Tommy Lasorda	30
2	Whitey Herzog	30
3	**Sparky Anderson**	27
4	Earl Weaver	22
5	Billy Martin	21
6	Dick Williams	18

Most LCS Games Won

1	Tommy Lasorda	20
2	**Sparky Anderson**	18
3	Whitey Herzog	18
4	Earl Weaver	15
5	Dick Williams	9
6	Tony La Russa	9

Cincinnati's Top Five Managers

		W	L	Pct.
1	**Sparky Anderson**	863	586	.596
2	Bill McKechnie	747	632	.542
3	Jack Hendricks	469	450	.510
4	Fred Hutchinson	446	375	.543
5	Pat Moran	425	329	.564

Detroit's Top Five Managers

		W	L	Pct.
1	Hughie Jennings	1131	972	.538
2	**Sparky Anderson**	895	777	.535
3	Bucky Harris	516	557	.481
4	Steve O'Neill	509	414	.551
5	Ty Cobb	479	444	.519

A Tribute
by Dan Ewald

September 10, 1989, is a day Sparky Anderson will remember for the rest of his life.

Even though it came during Sparky's most dismal year as a major league manager, it will always remain very special. That it did occur during such a disappointing season for the Tigers only helped to highlight how truly special it was.

That was the day Governor James J. Blanchard declared to be "Sparky Anderson Day" throughout the state of Michigan. There was a brief celebration on the field before the Sunday afternoon game with the Chicago White Sox followed by a reception to honor Sparky after the game.

On September 26, 1989, the day after the Tigers had suffered their hundredth loss of the season, the Tigers announced that Sparky's contract had been extended through the 1992 season.

"I've got to be the only manager in history to have a day named in his honor by the governor and also get a contract extension after a hundred losses," Sparky cracked lightheartedly after the season ended.

No doubt he is. But it really isn't surprising. In fact, nothing Sparky does or that happens to him should come as a shock to anyone.

Sparky Anderson is the one and only. He's a throwback to the days when baseball was played hard . . . when managers and players were like cartoon heros. He attacks every day with bounce and gusto, refusing to live in the past. And he's a visionary who's unafraid of the future, waiting—at times impatiently—to jump head and feet into it.

Sparky is Sparky. There isn't another one like him. With his zest for the game, his insight into people, his compassion for everyone around him, and his gift for gab, Sparky has established himself as baseball's old philosopher. He's become the yardstick by which all other managers are measured.

His star shines brightly atop the baseball galaxy. Yet he's as down to earth as a handful of hearty Kansas dirt. With his grandfatherly insight and his ability to touch so many people, he's the closest thing to Willie Nelson baseball has to offer.

The inscription on the proclamation from the governor pretty much tells the story: "Adored by children throughout the state, admired by his colleagues and cheered by his fans, Sparky Anderson is a true legend."

All true . . . yet terrifically understated.

Early in the season in 1987, Sparky made one of his regular visits to Children's Hospital. He's done this quietly throughout his career, dating back to his days at Cincinnati. There's never any fanfare; Sparky refused to let the media know anything about his visits.

These visits bring a little cheer to kids who are fighting a bigger battle in life than any three-game series with the Oakland Athletics. Sparky arranges for pizza to be delivered to all the kids. Then he visits as many rooms as possible once a week, merely trying to bring a smile to all those who are less fortunate. This probably means more to Sparky than it does even to those kids.

That one day, however, something special happened. One of the kids Sparky visited happened to be the son of a friend. The child had cancer, and Sparky spent the next couple of weeks frantically searching his mind to come up with something special he could do for hospitalized kids, particularly those whose families are financially hurting.

Sparky did come up with something, and it's grown into a program even larger than he could have imagined. Sparky created a charity called CATCH. It stands for Caring Athletes' Team for Children's and Henry Ford Hospitals. Sparky started it with a sports memorabilia auction that generated about $150,000. Items auctioned came from athletes all over the country and all were personally obtained by Sparky.

CATCH now has initiated a variety of fund-raising events and all are personally directed by Sparky. In just a few short years, CATCH has generated more than half a million dollars, and Sparky personally sees to it that all money goes directly to the kids. No red tape.

Sparky is a complicated contradiction of a person who thrives in the spotlight, yet longs for the privacy of his family and closest friends.

His energy for life and everyone and everything he touches is boundless. His enthusiasm is greater than a sixteen-year-old who just got his license to drive. From early morning until long past game time, Sparky rambles through life as if there were a TV camera focusing on him twenty-four hours a day.

Often there is. And Sparky makes sure to give time to everyone. He's so conscious of the media and the job it has to do, he makes sure to give every reporter a story that's a little bit different than the last interview he gave.

It doesn't stop with the media, however. That immeasurable energy extends to all baseball fans and every person he meets. Never does Sparky encounter an adoring fan who he doesn't stop to visit. If that fan happens to be a child, that youngster is in for the treat of a lifetime.

That's the amazing thing about Sparky. With his snow-white hair and chiseled rock features, he is more instantaneously identified than many movie stars. Somehow, however, he always manages to make time for fans. Rich or poor . . . black or white . . . young or old . . . it doesn't matter one bit. Sparky has time for everyone, often at the expense of his own well-being.

Sparky has done things to our language that would make most English teachers turn their heads into cue balls. But he's one of the greatest communicators this game has ever produced.

That's simply because Sparky knows people. He knows what makes them tick and he senses their pain when something deep inside is hurting. If he can soothe that pain by allowing them to talk with a major league manager for even just a few moments, he feels a compelling obligation to do so and simply does not know how to say no.

Make no mistake about it, Sparky loves the limelight. But he never forgets the tremendous responsibility that accompanies his celebrity. He's been compared to Casey Stengel—a comparison of the highest order for Sparky. But it probably falls short of all the good he has generated both on and off the field.

Because of his managerial success and those unmistakable physical features, Sparky is one of the most sought-after personalities for commercials and various appearances. Yet his primary focus remains his wife, Carol, and his family, and the game of baseball, to which Sparky owes his entire life.

Success in baseball, as in any walk of life, doesn't just happen. It's the result of blood, sweat, and tears. Sparky's phenomenal success in the 1970s at Cincinnati has been followed by a decade of excellence with the Tigers in Detroit.

He's been named Manager of the Year in both the National and

American Leagues. He is the only manager in history to win 800 games with two different teams. He's the only manager in history to win a World Series in both leagues. He ranks in baseball's top ten for victories by a manager and winning percentage.

Sparky would never admit it. But he's a sure-shot Hall of Famer as soon as he takes off that uniform for the final time.

Baseball is the vehicle through which America has come to know Sparky Anderson. The game itself, however, is just one side of a very complicated man who remains quite simple.

Sparky Anderson gives thanks in this book for all the opportunities baseball has provided him and his family. Baseball ought to be even more thankful for being blessed by Sparky, "a true legend."

Index

A

Aaron, Hank, 196–198
Abbott, Jim, 245
Abdul-Jabbar, Kareem, 158
All-time team, 191–206
Alston, Walter, 82–83, 89, 91–
     94, 95, 101, 104, 155, 248,
     249
Anaheim Stadium, 230–231
Anderson, Albert, 131, 154
Anderson, Beverly, 54
Anderson, Billy, 54
Anderson, Carol, 12, 20–22, 24,
28, 32, 45, 46, 50, 107, 132,
161
Anderson, Carolyn, 54
Anderson, George, 154
Anderson, Lee, 131, 154
Anderson, LeeRoy, 54–55, 63
Anderson, Sharon, 54
Anderson, Shirlee, 128, 131
Anderson, Shirley, 54
Arlington Stadium, 237
Astrodome, 224
Astroturf, 224, 235
Atlanta–Fulton County Stadium,
     221–222

Index

B

Bair, Doug, 125
Balboa, Rocky, 226
Ballparks, 219–238
Basilio, Carmen, 211
Basketball, professional, 155
Batboy at USC, 59
Baylor, Elgin, 215
Being a man, 133
Bench, Johnny, 21, 76, 84, 93–94,
 121, 122, 133, 135, 170–172,
 175, 198–199, 205
Bergman, Dave, 125
Berra, Yogi, 209, 235
Best percentages, 249
Big Red Machine, 11, 119, 120, 168
Bird, Larry, 215
Blair, Paul, 204
Blanchard, James J., 251
Boggs, Wade, 174, 194–195
Borbon, Pedro, 173
Boxing, 210–213
Brenneman, Marty, 131
Brett, George, 67, 174, 194–195
Bridgewater, South Dakota, 54, 57, 63
"Broadway Billy." See Schuster,
 Billy
Brown, Jimmy, 214
Brubaker, Bud, 58
Bryant, Clay, 4–6, 208
Burick, Si, 80, 121
Busch Stadium, 227

C

Campbell, Jim, 18, 23, 25, 30, 32, 77,
 139, 211
Candlestick Park, 229
Canseco, Jose, 159, 160, 174

Carbo, Bernie, 68, 119, 136
Caring Athletes' Team for Children's
 and Henry Ford Hospitals,
 (CATCH), 241, 253
Carlton, Steve, 227
Carroll, Clay, 74–75, 116
Castillo, Marty, 125
Celebrity status, 45–46
Chance, Frank, 249
Children's Hospital, 18
Cincinnati, 9, 11
Cincinnati's Top Five Managers,
 250
Clark, Will, 229
Clarke, Fred, 249
Clemens, Roger, 25
Clemente, Roberto, 114, 175, 196–
 197, 204
Cleveland Stadium, 232
Clutch performer, 165
Cobb, Mickey, 21
Cobb, Ty, 109, 159, 160, 163, 184,
 233, 250
Coleman, Vince, 69, 228
Comiskey Park, 231
Communication, 74
Concepcion, David, 117, 121, 136,
 137, 195
Conduct, personal, 71–74
Conn, Billy, 211
Consolo, Billy, 19–20
Craig, Roger, 20, 126, 138,
 155
Cuellar, Mike, 115

D

Daly, Chuck, 21
Dark, Alvin, 96
Davis, Glenn, 224

Index

Dedeaux, Rod, 41, 59–61
Defense, checking, 68
Designated hitter, 93
Detroit's Top Five Managers, 250
DiMaggio, Joe, 109, 210, 235
Dodger Stadium, 225
Dorsett, Tony, 157
Doubleday, Abner, 67
Double switch, 90
Doyle, Denny, 118
Dressen, Charlie, 208
Driessen, Dan, 136
Dugout, managing in, 67
Durocher, Leo, 155, 248

E

Eastwick, Rawly, 68, 119
Eckersley, Dennis, 67
Education, 160
Elbow, broken, incident of, 44
Ellis, Dock, 227
Enthusiasm, 59
Equipment, 159
Evans, Darrell, 125
Evans, Dwight, 119
Ewald, Dan, 251–255

F

Family, 50
Fans, influence of, 220
Farm systems, 155–156
Father, 11
Faust, Bob, 5
Feller, Bob, 232
Fenway Park, 230
Fingers, Rollie, 96, 201–202
Fired, 127

Firing, reason for, 135
Fisk, Carlton, 119
Football, professional, 155
Ford Frick Award, 144
Fosse, Ray, 184
Foster, Alan, 184
Foster, George, 118, 121, 136, 170
Four Horsemen, 157
Franks, Herman, 133, 155
Frisch, Frankie, 106
Front office, running to, 84

G

Gaddis, Danny, 4
Gaetti, Gary, 174
Garcia, Mike, 232
Gardening, 45
Garvey, Steve, 173
Gehrig, Lou, 109, 160, 235
Gehringer, Charlie, 233
Geronimo, Cesar, 121, 136
Ghetto, 53–54
Giammati, Bart, 187–189
Gibson, Bob, 175–176, 200–201, 228
Gibson, Kirk, 123–124, 125, 140, 160, 196, 237
Giusti, Dave, 170
Goals, 36–37
Golf, 45, 215–216
Golf, professional, 156
Gomez, Preston, 204
Gossage, Goose, 123–124
Grammas, Alex, 71, 136, 137, 138, 140, 193
Greenberg, Hank, 233
Griffey, Ken, 121, 136, 227
Growing up, 53–64
Gullett, Don, 136, 206

Index

H

Hagler–Tommy Hearns fight, 211
Hall of Fame, 49, 104, 172, 184, 189
Handshake, 55
Happiest years, 140
Harris, Billy, 5
Harris, Bucky, 248, 250
Harvey, Doug, 9–10
Hebner, Richie, 114
Hendricks, Jack, 250
Henry Ford Hospital, 30
Hernandez, Willie, 17, 79, 125, 231, 234
Herrelson, Bud, 184
Herzog, Whitey, 69, 82–83, 89, 98, 134, 220, 249
High school sports, 58
Hitters' parks, 221
Hockey, professional, 155
Holtz, Lou, 73, 217
Hornsby, Rogers, 160
Hough, Charlie, 237
Houk, Ralph, 32, 140
House cleaning, 45
Hrbek, Kent, 174
Hubert H. Humphrey Metrodome, 234–235
Huggins, Miller, 103, 249
Hunch, playing a, 70
Hutchinson, Fred, 250

I

Impact players, 165

J

Jack Murphy Stadium, 228
Jackson, Bo, 157

Jackson, Reggie, 109, 166–168
Jackson, Shoeless Joe, 160
Jennings, Hughie, 149, 250
Jobs, off-season, 62
Johnson, Magic, 158, 215
Johnson, Walter, 159, 163
John, Tommy, 128
Jordan, Michael, 158, 215

K

Kaline, Al, 150, 229, 233
Kell, George, 138–139
Kelly, Tom, 99
Kingdome, 236–237
Kirby, Clay, 197
Kittle, Ron, 232
Knight, Bobby, 217
Koufax, Sandy, 151, 200–201
Kuntz, Rusty, 125

L

Lacy, Lee, 128
Lajoie, Bill, 16, 30, 32, 77
Lakers, L.A., 28, 215
Landis, Judge, 187
Larsen, Don, 106–107
La Russa, Tony, 21, 67, 72, 99, 249
Lasorda, Tom, 21, 97, 155, 249
Lemon, Bob, 133, 232
Lemon, Chet, 125
Leonard, Sugar Ray, 211
Leyland, Jim, 99
Livingood, Clarence, 18, 23
Lombardi, Vince, 2–3
Lopez, Al, 71, 249
Lopez, Aurelio, 125
Los Angeles, 57
Losing, 34, 47

Losing, effect of, 246
Louis, Joe, 212
Loyalty, 146
Lynn, Fred, 15

M

McCarthy, George, 21–22
McCarthy, Joe, 248, 249
McCovey, Willie, 94, 172, 175, 192–
    193
McEnaney, Will, 68, 119
McGee, Willie, 228
McGlothlin, Jim, 115
McGraw, John, 36, 83, 88–89, 101,
    103, 248, 249
McGwire, Mark, 174
McKechnie, Bill, 248, 250
Mack, Connie, 88, 103, 248, 249
McNally, Dave, 115
McRae, Hal, 117, 136
Manager of the Year Award, 86,
    254–255
Managing, elements of, 66
Mangual, Angel, 117
Mantle, Mickey, 105, 209, 235
Marichal, Juan, 200–201
Marquez, Gonzalo, 116
Marshall, Mike, 93
Martin, Billy, 96, 106, 220, 249
Mathis, Buster, 213
Mattingly, Don, 67, 160, 174
Mauch, Gene, 81–83, 86, 89, 90,
    91–92, 101, 104, 155, 248
May, Lee, 192, 222
Mays, Willie, 204
Mazeroski, Bill, 203
Media, 210
    after firing, 132
    combine, 78–79
    dealing with, 77, 113
    Detroit, 24
    Detroit press conference, 30
    relationship with, 49
    speculation on future, 134
Memorial Stadium, 229
Merritt, Jim, 115
Mikan, George, 157–158
Milner, John, 185
Milwaukee County Stadium, 234
Minor Leagues, 155
Mistakes of managers, 85, 113
Mitchell, Kevin, 229
Molitor, Paul, 160
Monaghan, Tom, 31, 32, 77, 211,
    241
Money and success, 145–148
Moose, Bob, 170
Moran, Pat, 250
Morgan, Joe, 76, 84, 119, 121, 132,
    133, 135, 170–172, 175, 185,
    193–194, 227
Morris, Jack, 14, 124, 125, 140, 206,
    224, 231
Most gratifying year, 240
Most LCS Games Managed, 249
Most LCS Games Won, 249
Most Valuable Player Award, 171
Most World Series Games Managed,
    249
Most World Series Games Won, 249
Mr. Nice Guy Award, 106
Muhammad Ali, 211–213
Munson, Thurman, 122
Murtaugh, Danny, 197

N

Namath, Joe, 214
NCAA Tournament, 148

New York Baseball Writers Dinner,
106
Nicklaus, Jack, 216
Noll, Chuck, 227

O

Oakland Coliseum, 236
Oliver, Al, 114
Olympic Stadium, 225–226
O'Malley, Peter, 144
O'Neill, Steve, 250
Oquendo, Jose, 228
Overmanaging, 70
Ozark, Danny, 95

P

Pacific Coast League, 39
Painting, 44
Palmer, Arnold, 216
Palmer, Jim, 115
Parker, Wes, 202–203
Parrish, Lance, 125, 140, 196
Payton, Walter, 157, 214
People, being nice to, 55
Pepe, Phil, 107
Percentages, best, 249
Perez, Tony, 84, 93, 121, 170–172
Performance, 35
Petry, Dan, 125
Philadelphia, 219
Phillips, Lefty, 61, 95, 208
Pitchers' parks, 221
Pitcher, watching, 71
Post, Wally, 200
Poverty, 61
Professional contract, first, 61
Puckett, Kirby, 174

R

Rader, Doug, 203
Reagan, Ronald, 144
Record, 247–250
Religion, 36
Richard, J. R., 175
Rickey, Branch, 155
Ripken, Cal, 195
Riverfront Stadium, 223–224
Robinson, Brooks, 112, 115
Robinson, Jeff, 15
Rock Hill, 8
Rooney, Art, 227
Rose, Pete, 84, 89, 109, 119, 121,
133, 166, 168–169, 170–172,
175, 179–190, 199–200, 210,
227
Royals Stadium, 233
Rudi, Joe, 116
Russell, Bill, 93
Ruth, Babe, 102, 160, 163, 209, 229,
235
Ryan, Nolan, 159

S

Salary, average, 161
Sanguillen, Manny, 114
Schembechler, Bo, 73, 146–147, 216
Scherger, George, 70–71, 136
Schmidt, Mike, 220
Schofield, Dick, 231
Schuster, Billy, 39–41, 51
Scully, Vin, 21, 143
Sharman, Bill, 60
Shea Stadium, 226
Shepard, Larry, 137
Shore, Ray, 116–117, 120
Simmons, Ted, 173, 184, 234

Index

Simpson, Wayne, 115
Skydome, 237–238
Smith, Bill, 6–7
Smith, Dean, 147, 217
Smith, Ozzie, 175, 195, 203–204
Smith, Reggie, 46
Southworth, Billy, 249
"Sparky Anderson Day," 251
Spitz, Mark, 199
Sports, 58–60
Stargell, Willie, 114, 172, 196–197, 227
Staubach, Roger, 215
Stengel, Casey, 50, 78, 82–83, 97, 101–103, 106–109, 198, 210, 235, 240, 248, 249, 254
Strategy, 69
Success, 143–152
Successful person, philosophy of, 152

T

Talking a player down, 81
Tanana, Frank, 32
Tanner, Chuck, 21
Tarkenton, Fran, 214
Tate, Lee, 7–8
Television, influence of, 155
Templeton, Gary, 228
Tenace, Gene, 117
Tennis, professional, 156
Three Rivers Stadium, 227
Tiger Stadium, 232
Tommy Trojan Award, 60
Torre, Joe, 228
Tracewski, Dick, 138
Trammell, Alan, 15, 16, 125, 138, 140, 174, 195–196
Travel, 44

Trebelhorn, Tom, 99
Trevino, Lee, 145
Triple switch, 90

U

Understanding, 74–77
Understanding players, 84
Unitas, Johnny, 214
University of Southern California, 41

V

Veterans Stadium, 226–227

W

Wagner, Dick, 128–130, 135
Wagner, Honus, 160
Walker, Herschel, 157
Weaver, Earl, 249
Welcome home, 33
Whitaker, Lou, 125, 138, 140, 235
Wilcox, Milt, 125
Wilkens, Dominique, 158
Williams, Dick, 21, 123, 155, 249
Williams, Ted, 150, 230
Wilson, Flip, 45
Wilson, Willie, 205
Winaholic, a, 1, 47
Winfield, Dave, 166, 169–170, 174
Winning, 1–12
  no longer obsession, 244
  as obsession, 3
Winningest Managers, 248
Wockenfuss, John, 16
Wooden, John, 148, 217

Index

World Series, 109–126
  Cincinnati vs. Baltimore, 1970,
    114–115
  Cincinnati vs. Boston, 1975, 118–
    120
  Cincinnati vs. New York, 1976,
    120–123
  Cincinnati vs. Oakland, 1972,
    115–118
  Detroit vs. San Diego, 1984, 123–
    126

Wrigley Field, 222–223
Wynn, Early, 232

Y

Yankee Stadium, 235–236

Z

Zimmer, Don, 155